Monitoring and Controlling the International Transfer of Technology

James Bonomo
Julia Lowell
John Pinder
Katharine Webb
Jessie Saul
Peter Cannon
Jennifer Sloan
David M. Adamson

Prepared for the
Office of Science and Technology Policy

Critical Technologies Institute

RAND

Directly or indirectly, the federal government funds and thus subsidizes a significant amount of research and development that has potential economic value. These subsidies are intended in part to benefit U.S. firms and citizens. However, when the fruits of federally supported research and development are transferred overseas, U.S. citizens may lose these intended benefits.

This project examined the effectiveness of U.S. policies for controlling the international transfer of technology developed with federal support. It was conducted at the request of the White House Office of Science and Technology Policy and funded by the National Science Foundation through the Critical Technologies Institute's (CTI's) research contract.

This book reports the results of this examination of government policies. It provides a framework for understanding the economic significance of these policies and details the agency-specific measures that have evolved over several decades for limiting and controlling international technology transfer. It also compares U.S. policies with those of selected other industrialized nations. This work should be of interest to those concerned with international flows of technology, as well as those concerned more directly with U.S. policies involving both intellectual property and also cooperative agreements between industry and the federal government.

CTI was created in 1991 by an act of Congress. It is a federally funded research and development center sponsored by the National Science Foundation and managed by RAND, a nonprofit corporation created for the purpose of improving public policy. CTI's mission is to help improve public policy by conducting objective, independent research and analysis on policy issues which involve science and technology in order to

- Support the Office of Science and Technology Policy and other Executive Branch agencies, offices and councils,

- Help science and technology decisionmakers understand the likely consequences of their decisions and choose among alternative policies, and

- Improve understanding in both the public and private sectors of the ways in which science and technology can better serve national objectives.

CTI research focuses on problems of science and technology policy that involve multiple agencies. In carrying out its mission CTI consults broadly with representatives from private industry, institutions of higher education, and other nonprofit institutions.

Inquiries regarding CTI or this document may be directed to:

Bruce Don
Director, Critical Technologies Institute
RAND
1333 H St., N.W.
Washington, D.C. 20005
Phone: (202) 296-5000
Web: http://www.rand.org/centers/cti/
Email: cti@rand.org

CONTENTS

TABLES

This report focuses on the policies and procedures of the U.S. government concerning the international transfer of technologies in which the government has invested. It examines the economic effects of such transfers, the policies and practices of selected U.S. government agencies, and the policies and practices of several other advanced nations.

ECONOMIC EFFECTS OF INTERNATIONAL TECHNOLOGY TRANSFER

Our review of the economic effects associated with international technology transfers showed that it is extremely difficult to estimate the financial effect that these technology transfers have on the United States. Indeed, the information required to trace the interpersonal interactions that are a key method of technology transfer does not exist and probably never will. Even information that does exist in principle, such as the involvement of particular technologies in a joint venture, is difficult to gather. Doing so would be complicated by the inherent need to involve the private sector, which tends to view such information as highly proprietary. For these reasons, any assessment of the economic importance of international transfers is unreliable.

The economic analysis also raises an even more important point: The very methods of technology transfer that the U.S. government might seek to restrict internationally are also the principal source of valuable societal returns within the United States. Indeed, the potential for domestic benefits is precisely the rationale for governmental involvement in the development of selected technologies in the first place. Consequently, the U.S. government should be very hesitant to place restrictions on certain methods of technology transfer that might inadvertently eliminate valuable domestic benefits. Because of the risks associated with restricting international technology transfers and the difficulty of monitoring such transfers, we are recommending no major shifts in U.S. policy on this issue.

INTERNATIONAL AND COMMERCIAL INSIGHTS

Across many nations of the Organization for Economic Cooperation and Development (OECD), efforts are under way to spur economically important innovations. These international efforts are broadly similar, in that they center on various cooperative agreements, or partnerships, between national agencies and private firms within the nation. Outside of the United States, the focus is primarily on the economic benefits provided by these programs, rather than on the detailed tracing of the intellectual property created within government-industry partnerships. In many ways, this approach seems similar in philosophy to that arising within U.S. industry, where technology is seen as an asset to be used or traded for economic gains. More broadly, the emphasis in most nations is on enhancing the entire national innovation system, from tax laws to education. Technology development is only a small, though important, part of the whole effort. In part, this focus on other aspects of technology transfer may simply be a recognition of the difficulty of tracing technologies from their inception to their implementation in actual products.

AGENCY POLICIES

The individual agencies of the federal government do not view international technology transfer issues as central to their institutional missions. They largely handle such matters as a constraint. These agencies are usually guided by their overall goal or mission—such as the exploration of space or the improvement of human health—which often has little connection to technology transfer or its consequences. As a result, in fulfilling their obligations to monitor technology transfers, agencies usually emphasize the most easily monitored and counted aspects of technology transfer. These include the licensing or use of patents in which the federal government has an interest and the involvement of foreign firms in cooperative agreements of various sorts. Individual agencies do, however, have significant differences in their legislative mandates that affect their policies, particularly with respect to foreign firm participation in cooperative agreements. Currently, and perhaps because of these legislative differences, there is no formal interagency coordination on the issue of international technology transfer other than the national security process, which is driven by quite different concerns.

POLICY IMPLICATIONS

Given these findings, only a few small changes in the law and policy seem worthwhile. One sensible change would be to allow the protection and private use of "trade secret" type intellectual property created at the National Aeronautics and Space Administration (NASA) and perhaps also at the National Institutes of Health and within the Department of Defense as well. Currently at NASA, such information must be publicly disclosed, so its benefit cannot be restricted to U.S. firms. A second useful change would be to expand the Bayh-Dole Act requirement for "substantial" U.S. use of a patent when used for sales in the United States to include *assignments* of patents, in addition to simple licenses. Currently, while a U.S. firm might not be able to license a patent to a foreign firm, the U.S. firm may be bought by a foreign firm and so assign its licenses to its new parent firm. While entirely legal, this appears to circumvent the intent of the act. Given the small number of cases, this is more an issue of fairness than economic necessity. Third, an interagency effort could coordinate the decisions by individual agencies on the international reciprocity required for the various cooperative agreements, perhaps suggesting common definitions or even suggesting appropriate changes in some laws.

Overall, these changes are consistent with the position now emerging among many groups—an emphasis on all aspect of national innovation, rather than just on technological issues. While these steps would enhance the U.S. government's ability to trace and to capture the benefits of certain technical innovations, they would stay entirely within the existing set of limitations, centered on definable bits of intellectual property and access to cooperative agreements. This is different from expanding those limits to include other aspects of technology transfer, such as personnel movements or international joint ventures. Moreover, these efforts could support a diplomatic effort to coordinate international rules on intellectual property and access to cooperative programs.

In contrast with these small measures, larger changes that might at first appear attractive in fact pose significant problems. For example, comprehensive data-gathering efforts aimed at monitoring technology transfers through personal and professional interactions have little realistic potential to provide sufficient information to be useful in economic analyses. At the same time, however, the mere presence of such activity could inhibit desirable domestic transfers. Similarly, the creation of a large interagency process might appear desirable, since it would allow diplomatic and other issues to be taken into consideration in decisions regarding the participation of foreign firms in cooperative agreements. However, in the absence of changes in the underlying laws, the constraints facing each agency will remain heterogeneous, making a large interagency process of little use.

The authors could not have produced this document without the willing help of many people both inside the federal government and out. We appreciate their time and patience in explaining their agency or country's policies and practice. In particular, we would like to thank the following individuals:

Brian C. Belanger, Deputy Director, ATP, National Institute of Standards and Technology; Mark Bohannon, General Counsel, Department of Commerce; Connie K. N. Chang, Special Assistant to the Director, ATP, National Institute of Standards and Technology; Julia A. Conley, Supervisory Special Agent, Federal Bureau of Investigation; Jose M. Costa, Counselor, Science, Technology, and Education, European Commission; Nicholas Davidson, First Secretary (Trade Policy), British Embassy; William J. Denk, Director, Defense Programs Division, Export Administration (BXA), Strategic Industries/Economic Security; June W. Edward, Associate General Counsel, Commercial, NASA Headquarters; Gilbert Fayl, European Commission; Roy Forey, Science and Technology Officer, British Embassy, Washington, D.C.; M. Christina Gobin, Evaluator, National Security and International Affairs Division, U.S. General Accounting Office; Steven C. Goldman, Department of Commerce; Scott Harper, Supervisory Special Agent, Federal Bureau of Investigation; Paul J. Haurilesko, Evaluator, National Security and International Affairs Division, U.S. General Accounting Office; Nancy L. Hindman, Defense Technology Security Agency, Department of Defense; Kazuhiko Hombu, Chief Representative, Washington NEDO; Martin Kennedy, Attaché Defence Supply, Defence Supply Office, British Embassy, Washington, D.C.; John Konfala, DTSA/PD/AC&PA, Defense Technology Security Agency, Department of Defense; Anne-Marie Lasowski, Senior Evaluator, National Security and International Affairs Division, U.S. General Accounting Office; Richard Luetchford, Attaché Defence Equipment/IPR, British Embassy; Robert W. Maggi, Office of Arms Transfer and Export Control Policy, U.S. Department of State; John G. Mannix, Associate General Counsel, Patent & IPR, NASA Headquarters; Elizabeth A. Marini, DTSA/PD/AC&PA (Munitions), Defense Technology Security Agency, Department of Defense; Jon Paugh,

Department of Commerce; John Richards, Deputy Assistant Secretary of Commerce, Department of Commerce; Don A. Rolt, Counsellor, Science and Technology, British Embassy; Theodore J. Roumel, CRA, Assistant Director, Office of Technology Transfer, National Institutes of Health, U.S. Public Health Service; Rosalie T. Ruegg, Director, Economic Assessment Office, ATP, National Institute of Standards and Technology; Michael G. Snyder, Program Officer for Japan and China, Division of International Relations, National Institutes of Health; Jack Spiegel, Director, Division of Technology, Development and Transfer, National Institutes of Health; Peter Sullivan, Deputy Director, Defense Technology Security Agency, Department of Defense; James K. Swanson, DTSA/TSO, Defense Technology Security Agency, Department of Defense; Dave Tarbell, Director, Defense Technology Security Agency, Department of Defense; Scott C. Williams, Supervisory Special Agent, Federal Bureau of Investigation; Phyllis Yoshida, Director, Office of International Technology Policy, Department of Commerce; and Karen S. Zuckerstein, Assistant Director, National Security and International Affairs Division, U.S. General Accounting Office.

While this work could not have been produced without their help, the authors alone are responsible for any remaining errors.

ACDA	Arms Control and Disarmament Agency
AEC	Atomic Energy Commission
ATP	Advanced Technology Program
BXA	Bureau of Export Administration
CCL	Commodity Control List
CD-ROM	Compact disk read-only memory
CFR	Code of Federal Regulations
CRADA	Cooperative R&D Agreement
CTI	RAND's Critical Technologies Institute
DARPA	Defense Advanced Research Projects Agency
DEAR	Department of Energy Acquisition Regulations
DoC	Department of Commerce
DoD	Department of Defense
DoE	Department of Energy
EC	European Commission
HHS	Department of Health and Human Services
ITAR	International Transfer in Arms Regulations
LANL	Los Alamos National Laboratory
NACA	National Advisory Committee on Aeronautics
NASA	National Aeronautics and Space Administration
NEDO	New Energy and Industrial Technology Development Organization
NIH	National Institutes of Health
NIST	National Institute of Standards and Technology
NSB	National Science Board
NSF	National Science Foundation
NTIS	National Technical Information Service
OECD	Organization for Economic Cooperation and Development
OIDA	Optoelectronics Industry Development Association
OMB	Office of Management and Budget
PHS	Public Health System
PTO	Patent and Trademark Office

R&D	Research and Development
RaDiUS	Research and Development in the United States
SIC	Standard Industry Code
URL	Universal Resource Locator

Chapter One

INTRODUCTION

Over the past decade, substantial changes have occurred in both the international economic and the defense environments confronting the United States and other nations. In the development of new technologies, these changes have had profound effects in both industry and in government. Global competition in the marketplace and the fast pace of technological innovation have pushed commercial firms to focus relentlessly on their core capabilities. Consequently, longer-term research has been reduced in many areas. At the same time, the rapid evolution of technologies in the commercial sector has left the defense establishment far behind in important industries, such as microelectronics and software.

Many of the industrialized nations of the Organization for Economic Cooperation and Development (OECD) have adopted quite similar responses to these pressures. Across these countries, there are increasing numbers of government-industry partnerships for the development of selected technologies. The argument that is usually used to justify a government role in such programs is that the potential benefits to society of the technology are significant, while the private economic gains are both uncertain and difficult to appropriate, such that individual firms would not be willing to invest in the technology without government assistance. The government usually retains some control over the intellectual property generated by these joint efforts, although the importance attached to that control varies across nations.

The rapid pace of commercial innovation has also compelled the defense industry to concentrate on the "spin on" of commercially developed technologies and has contributed to an increasingly integrated dual-use technology base. As a result, the defense industry also depends, in part, on new government-industry partnerships.

A natural question is whether participation in a government-industry partnership should be limited to firms of the nation supporting it. In the United States, many of the statutes that have set up these programs answer this through an attempt at *reciprocity.* Reciprocity here means an equality of access—access for firms of another nation to programs in the United States balanced by access for U.S. firms to programs in that other nation. Most notably, this is the case for the Advanced Technology Program (ATP), which is administered by the National Institute of Standards and Technology (NIST). Some observers question the utility of such restrictions, as is evident in the following statement in a recent report by the Committee on Foreign Participation in U.S. Research and Development of the National Academy of Engineering:

> The committee considers the potential benefits of reciprocity requirements to be small and more than offset by the costs and risks they entail. Such requirements contradict stated U.S. foreign policy objectives, undercut U.S. efforts to persuade other nations to move toward unconditional nondiscriminatory treatment, and encourage U.S. trading partners to introduce similar requirements. (Reid and Schriesheim, 1996b, p. 11.)

Nonetheless, reciprocity requirements for foreign industrial participation in federally funded programs remain an important constraint across the U.S. government agencies we examined.

Another commonly used technology transfer restriction involves patents. Most patents with governmental involvement now follow the pattern of the Bayh-Dole Act (P.L. 96-517) and so require "substantial" use within the United States if the resulting sales are made within the United States. The implementation of this constraint, as well as those for cooperative agreements, has been left to the individual agencies or, in some cases, particularly those dealing with the oversight of patents, to their grantees or contractors.

Clearly, the results of such government-industry partnerships are only one element of a national innovation system. Other aspects, from tax laws to the supply of highly trained labor, are also important for the ultimate goals of a competitive industrial sector and a technologically advanced military. Any policy on innovation through technology development must keep this larger context in view, as indeed some policy treatments do. This report, however, focuses more narrowly on the mechanisms of international technology transfer, the challenges associated with monitoring and restricting such transfers, and the relevant policies of U.S. government agencies, as compared to those of other industrialized nations.

ORGANIZATION OF THIS REPORT

This study examined the international technology transfer policies of the U.S. government and their effectiveness. It is essential to frame this examination by first asking how important these policies are for economic growth in the United States. This question is addressed in Chapter Two, "Economic Effects of International Technology Transfer." The chapter begins by describing the conventional economic interpretation of technology transfer. This interpretation involves many factors, some of which are difficult to determine, such as how quickly technology is inadvertently transferred or how much the technology is worth, per se. To explore the practical effects of these difficulties, the framework is applied to a specific industry: optoelectronics. This application was chosen to be of interest intrinsically and to illustrate more generally what is "knowable" about the economic effects of technology transfer.

Chapter Three, "Comparisons Across Agencies," describes the policies of the United States government involving international technology transfer. The chapter focuses on the international technology transfer policies of the six agencies that account for the bulk of federal R&D: the National Aeronautics and Space Administration (NASA); the Department of Energy (DoE); the National Institutes of Health (NIH); the NIST's ATP within the Department of Commerce (DoC); the National Science Foundation (NSF); and the Department of Defense (DoD). These policies have arisen over several decades, so it is important to ask whether they have kept pace with changes in the economic environment and whether or not there is sufficient coordination within the Executive Branch on technology transfer policies. Several distinct areas of governmental policy address international technology transfer. The most obvious area is the ownership of patents or other intellectual property produced with governmental support and any restrictions on the licensing or sale of such patents. Another key policy area is the regulation of foreign participation in government-industry partnerships. In addition to restricting direct technology transfers, limiting participation to U.S. firms may also indirectly reduce some less-formal transfer methods, such as those associated with casual interactions and personnel movements. The chapter examines the implementation of policies in both areas by the key U.S. government agencies that support commercial technology development.

Chapter Four, "International Insights," deals with another source of insights: the policies and practices of other industrialized nations. We investigated the policies of the United Kingdom, the European Commission (EC) , and Japan. Here, the most important point appears to be the construction of the issue in other nations, as compared with the United States. Not surprisingly, given differences in history and in current governmental expenditures for technology development, other nations see the problem differently. These views appear close to that evolving within private industry in the United States, which is briefly developed in Chapter Five, "A Brief Observation from the Commercial World."

The insights we drew from these different strands of analyses are brought together in Chapter Six, "Potential Changes in International Technology

Transfer Policies and Procedures." In general, we found that the inherent limitations of the economic data and the risk of inhibiting the desirable domestic transfer of these technologies make comprehensive monitoring appear impractical and unwise. For a limited set of easily traced technologies, such as those involving patents or trade secrets, there are potential gains from small improvements in current practices. There could also be useful improvements in the coordination of the regulations among cooperative agreements of various kinds. In contrast, the creation of a centralized process for international determinations of eligibility seems less promising because of the statutory diversity across agencies.

Chapter Two

ECONOMIC EFFECTS OF INTERNATIONAL TECHNOLOGY TRANSFER

To understand the importance of U.S. attempts to monitor, control, and limit international technology transfer, the economic effects of such transfers must be determined. Accordingly, this chapter defines the problem and then provides a framework for understanding the flow of technology generated by research and development investments. This framework involves many factors, some of which are difficult to determine, such as how technology is inadvertently transferred or how much the technology is worth, per se. In an effort to explore the practical effects of these difficulties, this framework is applied to the optoelectronics industry, with an emphasis on its advanced display component. This industry was selected as a case study because it is of interest intrinsically— because of its significant commercial potential and high level of international competition—and is intended to serve as an illustration of what is "knowable" about the economic effects of technology transfer. The optoelectronics case study is followed by a brief discussion of some concluding observations and their implications for international technology transfer policy.

DEFINING PROBLEMS ASSOCIATED WITH INTERNATIONAL TECHNOLOGY TRANSFER

The U.S. government subsidizes commercially oriented research and development (R&D) using taxpayer money to achieve various domestic objectives. Inevitably, some of the technology generated by subsidized R&D, embodied in intellectual, physical, or human capital, will "leak out," intentionally or unintentionally, to foreign companies or governments. These technology transfers may cause Americans to lose a portion of the social benefits created by commercial R&D subsidization.

Why might these benefits of subsidized R&D be lost? The U.S. government does not generally retain the rights to technologies generated by subsidized commercial R&D projects or demand recoupment from the organizations that perform the R&D.[1] The government does, however, expect its subsidies to benefit Americans—directly, because subsidy recipients are American, and indirectly, because taxpayers benefit from positive spillovers associated with the development of new technologies and the production of resulting products. When technologies generated by subsidized R&D go overseas, however, whether in the form of blueprints, capital machinery, or human know-how, Americans can lose the intended benefits.

The problem of lost benefits from international technology transfer can take two forms—undervaluation of technology and "spillovers" outside the United States.

Undervaluation of Technology

A subsidized technology may be transferred for less than its "true" market value. This is obviously true if the technology is leaked overseas via industrial espionage. It may also happen, however, if the developers sell the technology for a price that they perceive to be fair but that does not capture the full market value. When the U.S. government subsidizes the development of a technology by a private firm, it effectively increases that firm's rate of return on its own R&D investment. A firm in this situation may undervalue its subsidized technology if (1) information about the "true" value of the technology is expensive or difficult to obtain, and (2) the firm is a "satisficer" rather than pure profit maximizers.[2] If the buyer is foreign, the difference between the "true" market value and the "satisficing" value will reflect a net loss to U.S. citizens, in this case the government-subsidized U.S. developers of the technology. Of course, if the buyer is another U.S. firm, there is no net loss of benefits to the United States.

Spillovers

A second way that Americans can lose—and foreigners gain—the benefits of U.S. government R&D subsidies is when desirable spillovers are transferred overseas. The total social returns to R&D include important spillovers, in addition to the private market value of the technologies generated by the R&D. If the spillovers are positive, private firms will tend to spend too little on R&D, from a social point of view. Government subsidies boost the level of R&D in an

---

[1]This differs from usual practice in the defense industry, where the government retains the rights to most weapon system technologies.

[2]A *satisficer*, as opposed to an *optimizer*, seeks only to achieve some minimum level of one or more objectives, rather than maximizing a single objective. Thus, a firm that is a satisficer might be willing to accept an adequate, rather than the maximum, rate of return on its R&D investment. Firms may exhibit this type of behavior if they have objectives other than profit, such as revenues or market share, or if they are trying to spread their risks across multiple investments.

effort to increase these "external" benefits, which cannot be captured by the firm performing the R&D. If, however, the spillovers motivating the subsidies are associated with the actual performance of the R&D or the production of resulting goods and if either of these processes is transferred abroad, the social return to the U.S. on its investment will not be fully realized. In this manner, foreigners may capture some of the benefits created by the U.S. government's R&D investments.

THE ECONOMIC CONTEXT OF INTERNATIONAL TECHNOLOGY TRANSFERS

Determining whether the problem of international technology transfer is significant poses two conceptual difficulties. First, the value of a technology to its developer may differ from the value placed on it by another firm. Indeed, this difference in value is what provides the incentive for the sale of the technology. Given asymmetric information, in addition to technological and market uncertainties, it is just as likely—perhaps even more likely—that foreign firms pay too much for U.S. technology, rather than too little. Price data alone, however, do not allow us to discriminate between these possibilities. Even in the extreme case, in which technology is transferred overseas via industrial espionage, it may not be possible to quantify the value of the stolen U.S. technology. Second, much of the benefit of U.S. government R&D subsidies will be lost to Americans if desirable spillover benefits are transferred overseas with the technology. Unfortunately, the extent of the problem is largely unknowable since, by definition, spillovers are achieved through nonmarket transactions.

With these difficulties in mind, what then can be said about the tracking and valuing of technology in general, and government-subsidized technology in particular? The diagram in Figure 2.1 is a notional illustration of how public and private sector R&D generates new and improved technologies that provide both private and public benefits to the United States and to foreign countries. The easiest flows to track in this framework are the R&D expenditures, although in practice such estimates can prove to be quite challenging. The relationship between public and private R&D expenditures on the inflow side and valuable technologies on the outflow side is essentially a "black box": It is extremely difficult to link the value of new and improved technologies to specific R&D efforts, except at the most disaggregated level. Furthermore, there is no way to measure the share of value created specifically by government-subsidized R&D, other than through some problematic survey research techniques.[3] On the

---

[3]Popper (1995) provides a useful discussion of some of the problems associated with survey approaches to determining social benefits of R&D.

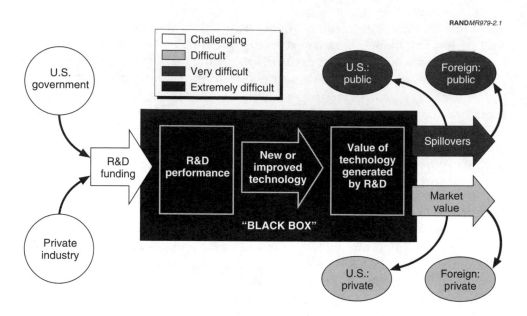

**Figure 2.1—Framework for Tracking the Development and
Transfer of New Technology**

outflow side, the market value of a technology can, with some difficulty, be estimated—either directly through its transfer price, or indirectly through the value
of products it generates. A similar approach can, in theory, be used to evaluate
the "external," or nonmarket, value of the spillovers associated with a technology. Unfortunately, such public benefits are very difficult to measure, since
they are not captured by market transactions.

ESTIMATING THE VALUE OF NEW TECHNOLOGY

Data that are both appropriate and reliable are a prerequisite for estimating the
value of technology transfers within the framework outlined above. Table 2.1
characterizes the availability of such data, based primarily on the data collection efforts associated with the optoelectronics case study. Even when the right
type of data is available, the conceptual difficulties of actually measuring the
value of a technology at a given stage of development remain.

Government R&D expenditure data are widely available but tend to take a considerable amount of time and effort to collect and process. Private R&D
expenditure data, based on an extensive survey by the Census Bureau, are
available from NSF but only at the broad Standard Industry Code (SIC) level
(NSF, 1993; NSF, 1994). More disaggregated data are not accessible because of
concerns about the disclosure of proprietary information.

Table 2.1

Availability of Data for Estimating the Value of Technology

	Source	Availability
R&D expenditures	U.S. government	Good
	Private sector	Moderate
Market value of technology	Profits from sales of related products	Poor
	Intentional technology transfers	Moderate
Social value of technology	Overseas leakages	Poor
	Spillover benefits	Poor

The discounted present value of future profits from related products provides a measure of the market value of a technology. Future profit estimates are, however, inherently uncertain; even if firms were able to make accurate estimates, they would probably be reluctant to release them. If a technology is intentionally transferred, a reasonable measure of its market value would be the price, or compensation, associated with the transaction. Of course, the transfer price is not inherent to the technology but rather depends on the future stream of profits that the buyer and seller expect to generate with it.

The social value of a technology, on the other hand, depends on the benefits that are accrued outside of the market, through spillovers and other leakages that are inherently difficult to measure. Even if useful measurement concepts could be devised (the market value of increased productivity might be one possibility), it would still be very difficult to obtain the type of data that is needed to quantify spillover benefits or technology leakages.

The preceding discussion has pointed out the difficulties associated with estimating the value of technology transfers. It is an even greater challenge to determine, with any confidence, the fraction of this value that is attributable to government subsidies. In addition, there are specific technology transfer mechanisms within each of the categories discussed above—intentional private transactions in the market context, and unintentional spillovers and leakages in the public arena—each with its own particular measurement difficulties and data availability challenges.

Estimating the Market Value of Intentional Technology Transfers

Technology can be transferred through four broadly defined market mechanisms:

1. sales of products that embody the technology
2. contractual arrangements, including licensing

3. cooperation and sharing among firms as part of a strategic alliance

4. acquisition and application of skills and know-how through direct investment.

These four mechanisms differ in a variety of ways that affect their measurability and the availability of measurement data, as characterized in Table 2.2.

It is fairly easy to measure technology transfers associated with the sales of producer goods that embody particular technologies. Detailed trade data are collected by the Census Bureau and are available from NSF (NSF, 1996). Technology is often transferred though a variety of contractual arrangements, of which licensing is the most common. These transfers can be measured easily if the terms of the transfer contract are known, but this information is not always available. Intentional transfers of human capital or know-how usually take place in the context of strategic alliances or direct investment by multinational corporations. These types of technology transfers are difficult to measure because they are nonmarket transactions, taking place between cooperating organizations or within a single organization.

Estimating Overseas Technology Leakages

Technology can sometimes be lost through unintentional "leaks," in which some or all of the essential elements of the technology are transmitted from one firm or person to another. The four categories of leakages considered here are

1. industrial espionage, often resulting in the outright theft of ideas, technical information, or strategies

2. reverse engineering of products embodying a technology

3. human capital movements, primarily through education and employment

4. information diffusion through professional publications and personal interactions.

The measurability and data availability for these leakage mechanisms are characterized in Table 2.3

Firms engaging in industrial espionage acquire the technology of another firm, then adapt it to gain some strategic advantage in the marketplace. The real cost of such transfers to the United States is not the profits earned by foreign firms using stolen technologies but rather the reduction in the profits of U.S. firms due to the thefts, together with any lost U.S. spillovers. This value is very difficult to measure, as there is no way to know what U.S. profits or spillovers would have been if a technology had not been stolen.

Table 2.2

Market Value of Intentional Technology Transfers

Transfer Mechanism	Measurability	Data Availability
Sales of producer goods	Easy	Good
Contractual arrangements	Easy	Moderate
Strategic alliances	Difficult	Poor
Direct Investment	Difficult	Moderate

Table 2.3

Overseas Leakages of Subsidized Technology

Type of Leakage	Measurability	Data Availability
Industrial espionage	Very difficult	Poor
Reverse engineering	Very difficult	Poor
Human capital movements	Difficult	Moderate
Information diffusion	Difficult	Poor

Many of the same measurement and data problems associated with industrial espionage also apply to reverse engineering, since this method of technology transfer usually requires some technical expertise and involves certain acquisition and adaptation costs. Indeed, case studies indicate that imitation lags can be quite significant (Mansfield et al., 1982).

Technology embodied in people can be transferred to other countries when students and researchers trained in the United States are hired by foreign firms. NSF survey data are available that track foreign graduate students, scientists and engineers working in the United States (NSF, 1996), but these data do not capture the value of their human capital or how much of that capital is transferred abroad. Visiting foreign scientists and engineers can also acquire technology during their stays in the United States and then transfer it back home. Anecdotal evidence suggests that short-term visitors are the most likely source of such transfers, while long-term visitors, like foreign graduate students, professors, and researchers, appear to be a net benefit to the United States (Reid and Schriesheim, 1996a).

Bibliometric methods, such as citation counts, can track the volume of technical information that is being exchanged or circulated, but they do not explicitly measure the value of the transfers associated with these information flows. Personal interactions at conferences and other professional meetings can also result in technology transfers, but these transfers go in both directions and are difficult to track.

Measuring the Spillover Benefits of R&D Investment

There are three broad categories of spillover benefits of R&D and the technologies it generates:

1. consumer surplus that is not captured in the price of new or improved products

2. externalities, both local and regional, associated with R&D and production facilities

3. inherent contributions to public goods, such as national security and public health.

Some attempts have been made to measure the first two of these three types of spillovers. For instance, Mansfield et al. (1977) calculated the increase in consumer surplus associated with technology improvements by estimating the area under the demand curve between the original price and the new lower price after an improved technology had been introduced. The data for these estimates were obtained through interviews with "innovating" firms. Jaffe (1986) estimated the spillovers created by R&D among firms that are technological "neighbors" using a model that predicted the success of an individual firm's R&D efforts, as measured by its patent filings and the market value of its new products. The data for this analysis were collected from the U.S. Patent Office and the Federal Trade Commission as part of a large study by the Harvard Business School. These two cases, and many others, illustrate how difficult it is to measure the real value of spillovers, although it is sometimes possible to isolate the locations that benefit the most. This general characterization is reflected in our evaluation of measurability and data availability with regard to spillovers, shown in Table 2.4.

Concluding Caveats

Finally, in considering these issues, two important caveats must be kept in mind:

1. Mechanisms for unintentional technology transfer are poorly understood, and there is little prospect for improvement.

2. Policies designed to inhibit unintentional transfers of technology abroad could discourage the domestic spillovers that motivate government subsidization of R&D in the first place.

Table 2.4

Spillover Benefits of R&D Investment

Type of Spillover	Measurability	Data Availability
Consumer surplus		
Value	Very difficult	Poor
Sales location	Difficult	Moderate
R&D and production externalities		
Value	Very difficult	Poor
Research location	Difficult	Moderate
Production location	Difficult	Moderate
Public good contributions		
National defense	Very difficult	Poor
Health and environment	Very difficult	Poor

A CASE STUDY OF THE OPTOELECTRONICS INDUSTRY

The following case study illustrates the economic framework depicted in Figure 2.1 by applying it to the optoelectronics industry, in an effort to estimate the value of optoelectronic technology attributable to government-subsidized R&D that is transferred abroad. The discussion of this case study begins with an overview of the various data sources that are available, followed by a discussion of how to define and bound the optoelectronics industry. Estimates of the level of R&D expenditures on optoelectronics in the private sector, and by the U.S. government, are presented next. With these estimates of the inputs to the technology generation "black box" in place, the technology outputs of the process can now be considered. Based on the limited data available about the optoelectronics industry, two broad areas of international technology transfer activity are examined:

1. Leakages of technology by U.S. firms active in foreign countries, through foreign business arrangements and the reverse engineering of technology embodied in products sold abroad.

2. Capture of spillovers and transfer of earnings abroad by foreign firms operating in the United States.

For each area of activity, a simple model of the value of U.S. government–subsidized technology transferred overseas is presented and then used to make very rough estimates of the magnitude of such transfers in the advanced display component of the optoelectronics industry. The application of these models illustrates the tremendous amount of uncertainty associated with their value estimates, while also indicating what data are needed to reduce that uncertainty.

Data Sources

This exploration of the optoelectronics industry drew upon a wide range of data, including funding, expenditure, and trade figures; descriptions of research projects; personal interviews; and analysis of industry surveys. These data were culled from a variety of different sources, which fall into two clear categories: specific studies of the optoelectronics industry and more general collections of R&D information.

Studies Specific to the Optoelectronics Industry. The *Critical Technology Assessment of the U.S. Optoelectronics Industry* (DoC, 1994) is centered around a survey of around 100 optoelectronics firms conducted in 1992 and 1993 by DoC, Bureau of Export Administration (BXA). The report contains a great deal of useful, though somewhat dated, information about the industry.

The *Optoelectronic Technology Roadmap* (1994), published by the Optoelectronics Industry Development Association (OIDA), examines market trends in the optoelectronics industry, identifies key technology areas, and makes recommendations regarding R&D strategies and priorities. Arpad Bergh, the President of OIDA, provided us with estimates of industry revenues and private R&D investment, as well as the level of funding for optoelectronic technologies from various federal government sources.

Optoelectronics at NIST (NIST, 1996) describes all of the projects at the NIST Laboratories that involve optoelectronics. The descriptions include funding source fractions, but not totals.

The Internet web site maintained by the NIST ATP, http://www.atp.nist.gov, provides access to specific optoelectronics information, as well as descriptions of ATP research awards that include dates and funding totals.

General R&D Information. RaDiUS® (Research and Development in the United States) is a database built and maintained by the Critical Technologies Institute (CTI) at RAND. It includes information on almost all of the R&D conducted or funded by the federal government, for FY 1994 through the present.

The CorpTech database (1996, Corporate Technology Information Services, Inc.), which is available on CD ROM and in printed form, includes survey data from almost all of the technology firms operating in the United States. The record for each firm contains reported information about ownership, product types, and estimated sales.

The tables in *Research & Development in Industry* (NSF, 1993; NSF, 1994) are based on annual Census Bureau survey data and include time series of total, federal, and private R&D funding and intensity. But since these data are aggregated by (three-digit) SIC, it is not possible to isolate the optoelectronics industry.

The *Science and Engineering Indicators 1996* (NSB, 1996) compilation contains a wide array of data from many different sources, including trade and patent information, classified by technology.

Globalizing Industrial Research and Development (Dalton and Serapio, 1995) provides an overview of industrial R&D activities in the United States, including the location and purpose of foreign-owned R&D facilities. In an informal interview, Dr. Dalton discussed his views on the implications of this foreign involvement in U.S. R&D.

Foreign Participation in U.S. Research and Development: Asset or Liability is the final report of the Committee on Foreign Participation in U.S. Research and Development of the National Academy of Engineering (1996). This document reviews the literature on this subject and integrates it with anecdotes, surveys, and informed opinions to support a series of recommendations.

Bounding the Optoelectronics Industry

An essential first step in this case study was to develop a broad definition of the optoelectronics industry. This enabled us to select a set of the firms, products, technologies, and R&D efforts that span this industry. The SIC codes are too broad to be useful for this task, so it is better to define the optoelectronics industry in terms of product types and technologies.

The OIDA *Optoelectronic Technology Roadmap* identifies and examines four categories, based on technology, within the optoelectronics industry: military, industrial, and consumer displays; optical communications (including optical computing); optical data storage; and hard copy. According to the president of OIDA, Arpad Bergh, additional technology categories, including sensors and components, are also important.

In this case study, we defined the optoelectronics industry broadly to include the three product-based categories[4]:

1. optoelectronic components

2. advanced military, industrial, and consumer displays

3. optical storage, computing, and communications equipment.

---

[4]Note that some, but not all, laser and electro-optic sensor technology is captured by one or more of these three categories.

An important conclusion can be drawn from this industry definition effort: It is best to focus on specific technology areas or products that are easy to identify and build up an industry in that manner.

U.S. Government R&D Expenditures

Six federal departments and agencies account for almost all of the optoelectronics-related R&D supported by the U.S. government. Estimates of the funding provided by these federal sources are shown Table 2.5. These data are quite informative, but some clarification and interpretation are necessary to place this information in the proper context.

The RaDiUS data in Table 2.5 include federal funding for R&D by all performers, within the government itself, as well as in the private and nonprofit sectors. The BXA survey, on the other hand, only includes federally funded R&D performed by private firms. This difference probably explains why the DoD is by far the largest source of federal funding in the BXA data, while other sources are much more prominent in the RaDiUS data.

Separate searches of the RaDiUS database were conducted to obtain funding figures for the three categories shown in Table 2.5. Thus, it is possible that some projects were counted in more than one category, so that the total funding across all three categories may be less than the sum of the amounts in each individual category. In addition, the search may have captured projects that do not really involve optoelectronics or involve it only peripherally. These overlapping and misidentified projects do distort the funding totals, but it would take considerable time and effort to find them and correct their effects.

The RaDiUS database search also provided information about where the funding indicated in Table 2.5 was directed within each government entity. Most of the DoE expenditures were in the form of Cooperative Research and Development Agreements (CRADAs) and of the discretionary funds allocated by the national laboratories. The NSF and, to a lesser extent, NASA fund an array of both basic and applied research in all aspects of optoelectronics, while most funding at the NIH is in the area of lasers and medical imaging. The principal funding sources at NIST and DoD were, respectively, ATP and the Defense Advanced Research Projects Agency (DARPA). The optoelectronics expenditures within these two programs are examined in greater detail, since they accounted for much of the total funding.

ATP. A total of 39 ATP awards were determined to involve optoelectronic technologies, based on the descriptions available at the ATP web site.[5] These

---

[5]URL: **http://www.atp.nist.gov**, last accessed March 1997.

Table 2.5

Federal Funding for Optoelectronics R&D ($ millions)

Funding Source	RaDiUS FY95			BXA Survey 1992–1995
	Optoelectronic Components	Advanced Displays	Optical Storage, Computing, and Communications	All Optoelectronics
National Institute of Standards and Technology	29.1	58.4	47.3	2.6
Department of Defense	34.2	85.8	99.9	185.8
Department of Energy	5.0	12.8	1.3	0.3
National Institutes of Health	0.8	5.0	13.1	1.0
National Science Foundation	29.0	6.2	20.7	0.3
National Aeronautics and Space Administration	1.3	0.4	0.5	6.3
Total	100.0	169.0	183.0	200.0

NOTES: This table includes data from two sources: the RAND-CTI RaDiUS database for Fiscal Year 1995 (first three columns); and a survey of the optoelectronics industry conducted by BXA in 1992 and 1993 (last column). It should be noted that the BXA numbers are averages over four years, three of which are projected estimates (1993, 1994, and 1995). The totals in the bottom row of the table are rounded up to the next nearest million dollars and may include some funding from sources other than those listed.

awards were all initiated between 1990 and 1995 and differed in their expected duration, with an average of three years. The total ATP funding for these awards was $143 million, with ATP matching the contributions of the participating firms. Thus, during this period, a typical ATP award involving optoelectronics was about $3.67 million, over three years, and the total annual ATP funding for all optoelectronics projects averaged about $44 million per year. It should be noted that this recent increase in optoelectronics R&D funding by ATP is captured by the RaDiUS data but not by the BXA survey.

DARPA. This defense agency is a major source of federal funding for optoelectronics R&D. According to the Arpad Bergh, the President of OIDA, DARPA will in FY97 have provided about $53 million in funding for display research alone and another $72 million for other optoelectronics R&D, mostly in components and communications.

Private-Sector R&D Expenditures

The results of the BXA survey of about 100 optoelectronics firms in 1992 and 1993, presented in the *Critical Technology Assessment of the U.S. Optoelectronics Industry*, include total R&D expenditures by firms in the optoelectronics industry, split between in-house (private) and government sources, as well as the

R&D intensity (R&D funding divided by sales revenues) in each product-customer category. Between 1989 and 1995, the total annual private R&D expenditures of the firms was in the range of $600 to 700 million. In 1991, the private funds represented 77 percent of total R&D expenditures on all optoelectronics and 70 percent of R&D on nondefense display products. In that same year, the private R&D intensity was 8.9 percent for all optoelectronics, and 14.0 percent for nondefense displays.

This aggregate information from the BXA survey, together with firm-level data from the CorpTech database, was used to make an estimate of the current level of private R&D in the advanced display segment of the optoelectronics industry. A set of CorpTech product categories associated with advanced display technologies was used to create a list of firms that sell those display products. These firms were divided into two groups: *specialized* and *diverse*. Specialized firms concentrate almost exclusively on display products, while diverse firms sell many nondisplay products. The total reported yearly sales for all of the display firms was $203 billion ($195 billion by the diverse firms and $8 billion by the specialized firms). The private R&D estimates in Table 2.6 were made using these sales totals. Each estimate is based on assumptions about private R&D intensity and on the share of sales generated by display products in specialized and diverse firms. Display sales were calculated for each group, multiplied by R&D intensity to determine private R&D expenditures, and aggregated to estimate the total private R&D. These calculations indicate that, based on the assumptions made, yearly private R&D expenditures in the area of advanced displays are somewhere between $1.0 and 5.5 billion, with a best guess of about $2.5 billion.

Transfers by U.S. Firms in Foreign Countries

There are essentially two means by which technology developed in the United States, with some measure of government support, can be transferred to foreign

Table 2.6

Private R&D Expenditures

Estimate		Lower	Middle	Upper
Private R&D intensity (%)		7.5	10	15
Specialized firms (224)	Total sales ($B)	8.00	8.00	8.00
	Display sales share (%)	50	70	90
	Private display R&D ($B)	0.30	0.56	1.08
Diverse firms (83)	Total sales ($B)	195.00	195.00	195.00
	Display sales share (%)	5	10	15
	Private display R&D ($B)	0.73	1.95	4.39
Total private R&D ($B)		1.03	2.51	5.47

countries by U.S. firms operating abroad. First, the U.S. firms that posses the government-subsidized technology, which can even include the expertise and know-how of individual employees, can voluntarily transfer this technology to foreign firms through a variety of business arrangements. A second, less voluntary means of transfer is the "leakage" of technology that can occur when the products of U.S. firms that in some manner embody a government-subsidized technology are sold abroad.

Foreign Business Arrangements. The BXA survey includes some data on business arrangements engaged in by U.S. firms in foreign countries or with foreign firms. Table 2.7 shows the number of firms involved in each of several different types of foreign business arrangements, along with the total number of each type of arrangement reported. The various types of arrangements used in the BXA data can be grouped into three categories, as follows:

1. Direct Investment
   - wholly owned subsidiaries
   - joint ventures

2. Strategic Alliances
   - membership in consortia and industry associations
   - participation in development of industry standards

3. Contractual arrangements
   - marketing, sales, and distribution agreements
   - product and process licenses

Table 2.7

Foreign Business Arrangements Engaged in by U.S. Optoelectronics Firms

Type of Arrangement	Number of Agreements	Number of Firms
Marketing/distribution	124	19
Licensing	36	14
Collaborative R&D	17	9
Joint venture	13	9
Supplier	9	6
Investor/subsidiary	6	5
Standardization	4	2
Consortia/memberships	3	2

SOURCE: BXA Optoelectronics Survey (1992–1993).
NOTE: The data in table are based on a total of 183 agreements reported by 50 of the firms participating in the survey

- collaborative research and joint product development
- cooperative agreements with suppliers.

Technology transfers in the context of direct investment and strategic alliances take place within a single firm or a larger organization and tend to be fairly informal. As a result, such transfers are generally more difficult to valuate and track than those associated with contractual arrangements, where expectations and interactions are more formal and tend to be captured more explicitly by market transactions.

It should be noted that no value was attached to the arrangements reported in the BXA survey data, and the direction of any transfer of technology was not indicated. Thus, a small number of strategic alliances and direct investment arrangements could potentially involve a considerable amount of technology transfer, especially if they draw heavily on the expertise of the firms involved. Also, even if there were a direct measure of the value of the transfers associated with these arrangements, it would still be difficult to determine their real significance. These transfers are intentional, and thus paid for, so real losses would only be incurred if the transfer moved beneficial spillovers abroad, or if the foreign recipient paid too low a price.

International Product Sales

It is very difficult to estimate the value of any technology transferred through product sales. A technology that is fully embodied in a product is acquired directly when the product is purchased. Other technologies can, with some level of previous knowledge, be reverse engineered from the products they are used to produce. The sales of both such products abroad can result in the international transfer of the technology associated with them.

The Census Bureau estimates that, in 1994, exports of "advanced optoelectronic products and components" were valued at about $0.9 billion.[6] The total estimated product sales of the firms participating in the BXA survey was $6 billion for 1995, but there was no indication in the survey of what fraction of those sales were international. A reasonable estimate of this international sales fraction, based on CorpTech data, is between 10 percent and 25 percent, implying that $0.6 to 1.5 billion of the 1995 revenues of the firms in the BXA survey were derived from foreign sales. Table 2.8 shows how estimates of international display product sales in 1996 are calculated. These calculations use an approach similar to the private R&D calculations in Table 2.6, relying on aggregations of

---

[6]This type of information is available in *Science & Engineering Indicators* (NSB, 1996).

Table 2.8

International Product Sales

Estimate		Lower	Middle	Upper
Specialized firms (244)	Total sales ($B)	8.00	8.00	8.00
	Display sales share (%)	50	70	90
	International sales share (%)	5	10	15
	International display sales ($B)	0.20	0.56	1.08
Diverse firms (83)	Total sales ($B)	195.00	195.00	195.00
	Display sales share (%)	5	10	15
	International sales share (%)	20	25	30
	International display sales ($B)	1.95	4.88	8.78
Total international display sales ($B)		2.15	5.44	9.86

CorpTech data on the total sales and international sales fractions of individual firms. These calculations yielded a range of roughly $2 to $10 billion worth of international display sales, with a middle estimate of about $5.4 billion.

The Census Bureau trade figures, and the international sales estimates based on BXA and CorpTech data, provide some indication of the value of optoelectronics products sold abroad but do not include the value of any transfers that are not captured by prices, much less any indication of the fraction of the value that is attributable to government funded R&D. Indeed, the large trade deficit in these products ($1.6 billion, for the Census Bureau optoelectronics category) indicates that transfers of this type may actually be a net benefit to the United States, since some foreign technologies are absorbed from imported products. Nonetheless, it is possible that some important government-subsidized technologies could be compromised through exports, thus making it worthwhile to think about how to estimate the magnitude of such losses.

The value of technology acquired by foreign firms through leakages, such as reverse engineering, associated with products sold abroad (T_{INT}) can be estimated with the following model:

$$T_{INT} = S_{INT} \cdot R_{INT} \cdot L,$$

where S_{INT} is the market value of products sold abroad by firms operating in the United States; R_{INT} is the fraction of the products' value that is attributable to federal R&D; and L is the value, as a fraction of sales, of any and all technology leakages to foreign firms through those products.

Figure 2.2 illustrates the range of estimates for T_{INT} generated by this model, based on the middle estimate of S_{INT}, $5.4 billion, from the international sales calculations shown in Table 2.8. The values of L and R_{INT} are both highly uncertain, so a contour plot is used to indicate the value of T_{INT} over plausible ranges of both parameters: 0 to 8 percent for L, and 0 to 16 percent for R_{INT}. Similar charts could be generated for the lower and upper estimates of the level of international sales, but these charts would differ only in scale from the chart shown in Figure 2.2.

This approach avoids making an exact estimate of the value of transfers but does show how valuable such transfers would be given different assumptions about (1) how much of a contribution federal R&D makes to the market value of products exported abroad, and (2) how much value is ultimately lost through such exports. If the midrange values of the parameters are accurate, the total value of display technology transfers through product sales abroad is roughly $15 to 25 million per year. The assumptions underlying this estimate, however, are merely best guesses. With more reliable data specific to the industry, this approach could provide a more conclusive estimate of the value of technology transfers through product sales abroad.

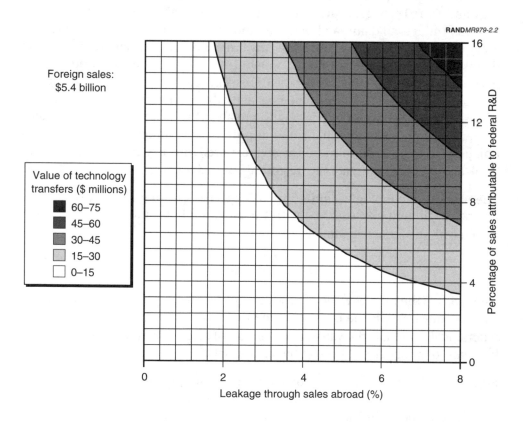

Figure 2.2—Estimated Value of Subsidized Display Technology
Transferred Abroad Annually Through Product Sales

Transfers to Foreign Firms Operating in the United States

There are a variety of ways that foreign firms operating in the United States can acquire technology that has been subsidized by the U.S. government. The most direct approach foreign firms can take is direct investment—the outright purchase of a U.S. firm enables the new foreign owner to absorb the technology of its new subsidiary directly, including technology generated by U.S. government R&D efforts. Foreign firms and their subsidiaries can also purchase technology from U.S. firms through intentional transfer mechanisms, such as contracts, licensing, and other arrangements. Foreign-owned firms may also obtain U.S. technology for little or no additional cost by taking advantage of the spillover benefits of operating in the United States, such as those that occur near cutting-edge research facilities at universities and government or private laboratories. These are, of course, the same spillover effects that benefit American firms and citizens and provide the primary motivation for many federal R&D subsidies. A real loss, however, does not occur unless the foreign-owned firms transfer the government-subsidized technologies they have acquired in the United States to their parent firms abroad, for use in the development, production, or sales of new products elsewhere to generate profits for foreign shareholders.

The percentage of all firms operating in the United States that are foreign-owned provides some indication of the potential for international technology transfers, especially those associated with spillovers. Table 2.9 shows the degree of foreign participation in the U.S. optoelectronics industry, as indicated by the number of firms included in the CorpTech database. The table suggests that the segments of the U.S. optoelectronics industry that should be of the most concern are those in which foreign-owned firms are most prevalent: entertainment, storage, and displays.

The concentration of foreign-owned firms is not, unfortunately, a direct measure of the value of spillover transfers. Moreover, the presence of foreign firms in the United States might actually be a net benefit, since these firms make unintentional contributions to the pool of spillovers available to all firms and may contribute more to that pool than they take from it. This is especially true when foreign firms acquire ailing U.S. firms and make them more productive than they would have otherwise been. Nonetheless, this type of information can provide clues about where transfers are likely to be the most significant.

The value of the technology absorbed by foreign firms operating in the United States through spillovers and earnings transferred abroad (T_{US}) can be estimated as follows:

$$T_{US} = S_{US} \cdot R_{US} \cdot [FO \cdot P + FI \cdot (1—P)] \, ,$$

Table 2.9

**Foreign Participation in the U.S.
Optoelectronics Market, as Indicated by
Number of Firms**

Category	Total Firms	Foreign Firms	Foreign Share (%)
Displays	308	63	20
Fiber optics	386	60	16
Storage	151	43	28
Lasers	405	68	17
Components	458	63	14
Measurement	284	39	14
Entertainment	19	6	32
All categories[a]	1,730	279	16

SOURCE: CorpTech database (1996), Corporate Technology Information Services, Inc.

[a]Some firms have products in more than one category, so the sum of the firms in each category will exceed the total number of firms in all seven categories.

where S_{US} is the market value of sales by foreign-owned firms operating in the United States; R_{US} is the fraction of the value of sales by foreign firms operating in the United States that is attributable to federal R&D; P is the profitability (profit/sales revenues) of foreign firms operating in the United States; FO is the fraction of foreign firm shares that are owned by foreigners; and FI is the fraction of input costs (labor, capital) that are paid to foreign firms and residents.

Table 2.10 shows the calculations used to estimate S_{US}, based on the total sales by foreign firms determined directly from the CorpTech data—$4.6 billion for specialized firms and $7.2 billion for diverse firms. These calculations indicate that the total annual display sales by foreign firms operating in the United States ranges from $2.7 to 5.2 billion, with a middle estimate of $3.9 billion.

Figure 2.3 presents a contour plot of T_{US} similar to the one shown in Figure 2.2 for T_{INT}. A range of 1 to 5 percent was selected for the profitability of foreign firms in the United States—the parameter on the x-axis of this plot—based on the results of the BXA Optoelectronics Survey, which indicated that the median profitability for display firms was about 1.5 percent. The y-axis parameter in the plot is R_{US}, the fraction of sales by foreign firms that is attributable to federal R&D. The range for R_{US} is 0 to 8 percent, which is half of the range for R_{INT} in Figure 2.2; foreign firms are less likely to be receiving direct federal R&D than U.S. firms, so one would expect that foreign firms gain less overall from U.S. government R&D than U.S. firms do. The plot uses the middle estimate of $3.9 billion for foreign firm display sales and assumes that 80 percent of foreign firm

Table 2.10

Display Sales by Foreign Firms Operating in the United States

Estimate		Lower	Middle	Upper
Specialized firms (244)	Total sales($B)	4.60	4.60	4.60
	Display sales share (%)	50	70	90
	Foreign firm display sales ($B)	2.30	3.22	4.14
Diverse firms (83)	Total sales($B)	7.20	7.20	7.20
	Display sales share (%)	5	10	15
	Foreign firm display sales($B)	0.36	0.72	1.08
Total foreign firm display sales ($B)		2.66	3.94	5.22

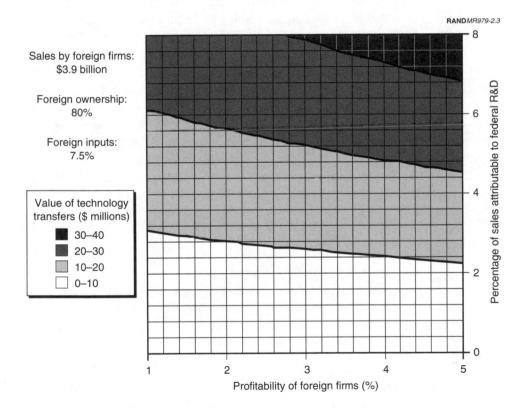

Figure 2.3—Estimated Value of Subsidized Display Technology Transferred Abroad Annually Through Spillovers Captured by U.S.-Based Foreign Firms

shareholders are foreign residents and that 7.5 percent of input costs are foreign. The midrange of the parameter estimates in this plot predicts that the value of U.S. spillover transfers of display technology to foreign firms is between $10 and 25 million per year.

Summary of Display Data and Estimates

The preceding estimates of R&D activity and the value of technology transfers involving government-subsidized display technology are only intended to be illustrative, since they rely on a wide array of plausible, though unverified, assumptions. With the appropriate degree of caution, these estimates can be viewed in the context of the technology tracking framework presented in Figure 2.1, in an effort to estimate the magnitude of international transfers involving technology generated by federal R&D efforts.

The total federal share of R&D in the display segment of the optoelectronics industry appears to be about 7 percent, where federal funding amounts to $170 million per year (see Table 2.5), and private expenditures are roughly $2.5 billion per year (see Table 2.6). The total sales of display products by all firms operating in the United States are estimated to be approximately $25 billion per year, based on reported sales in the CorpTech database. Of this total, international sales are estimated to account for $5.4 billion (see Table 2.8), and foreign-owned firms are estimated to account for around $3.9 billion (see Table 2.10). These R&D and sales estimates, together with a variety of other assumptions, yield a very rough "ballpark" estimate of the value of international transfers involving government-subsidized display technology. This ballpark total comes to $25 to 50 million per year—$15 to 25 million through the sales of U.S. products abroad and $10 to 25 million in the form of spillovers captured by foreign firms operating in the United States—which is equivalent to about 15 to 30 percent of all federal R&D expenditures in this segment of the optoelectronics industry.

There is, however, an extremely high degree of uncertainty in this estimate. It is very difficult to estimate confidently how much any technology transferred to foreign firms is really worth. It is also a tremendous challenge to determine what fraction of the value of a technology is attributable to R&D funded by the U.S. government. Indeed, it is difficult to even calculate the value of a technology by itself. Thus, the estimates presented here are largely speculative and highly uncertain.

Nonetheless, the exercise of making such estimates, based on the data available, is useful. It provides an opportunity to create and refine a methodology for determining the value, path, and extent of transfers involving technologies that were subsidized by the U.S. government. The development and application of this methodology serves to illustrate the deficiencies in the current data and the inherent limitations of various international technology-transfer measures.

One important insight can be drawn from this examination of the optoelectronics industry in particular: Private-sector cooperation and participation are essential for an accurate measure of technology transfer. Most firms in the display industry sell a variety of nondisplay products, so an accurate measure of the value of display technology would require the cooperation of individual firms to disaggregate display earnings from their total sales revenues and to specify the contribution from international sales. Firms are the best source of data on their own input expenses and profitability, and their active participation would be a vital component of research on the measurement of internal and collaborative transfers, as well as the links between government-subsidized R&D and the value of the new technologies that it ultimately generates.

CONCLUDING OBSERVATIONS ON ECONOMIC EFFECTS

The insights that can be drawn from both the economic analysis and the case study of the optoelectronics industry are consistent. First, they both showed that much economically important information is unavailable to decision-makers. Even such basic information as research spending is difficult to gather, because the private sector treats it as proprietary. Since most research is conducted by large firms with many product lines, determining inputs into a particular technology is difficult. Even with such information, the value of a technology is hard to determine; so much so, in fact, that many firms prefer to share technology through joint ventures rather than take the risk of selling a technology outright, precisely because the firms themselves have trouble determining the value of a given technology. Finally, many technologies are valued as a part of a greater whole, with firms using their portfolio of technical capabilities as a single, valued strategic asset. The value of the federal contribution to such an array is thus very difficult to estimate.

International transfers are inherently difficult to estimate as well. First, certain methods of transfer, such as espionage or personal contacts, are impossible to assess quantitatively. Second, the measurement of even ordinary mechanisms, such as reverse engineering, involves significant intrinsic uncertainties. The highly uncertain estimates in the optoelectronics case study indicate that largely unavoidable transfers could amount to 15 to 30 percent of federal R&D investments.

Whether this amount is large or small is a question of perspective. This percentage is lower than most estimates of the average social rate of return on private R&D investments, which range from about 50 to 100 percent. (Mansfield, 1977; Foster Associates, 1978; Robert R. Nathan Associates, 1978.) Even so, 30 percent is still a large percentage of the federal investment to be flowing overseas.

Most importantly, however, the mechanisms associated with many of these international transfers are identical to the methods of spillover that are so desirable in the domestic economy. It is precisely these unavoidable transfers that keep one firm from appropriating all the economic benefits of a technology, thereby creating the higher social rate of return that justifies government investment in the first place.

If the United States attempts to restrict such transfers, in an effort to limit the diffusion of technology overseas, it would run two risks. The first risk is that the desirable spillovers might be restricted as well. Given the apparently large role of essentially unmonitorable transfers—through personal contacts, espionage, and so on—it is probably imprudent to risk the domestic gains in an attempt to prevent such losses. The second risk is that restrictions aimed at preventing reverse engineering would require either extensive controls after sale or the forgoing of international sales. Neither approach appears to be a plausible path to international competitiveness.

POLICY IMPLICATIONS

Our analysis of the economic effects of international technology transfer suggests that it would be extremely difficult and impractical to develop a system for tracking and restricting such transfers. As we noted above, the necessary economic data in many cases do not exist or are difficult to obtain. The level of effort and resources required to implement such a system would not be justified by the expected gains. Furthermore, the detailed tracking of technology transfers, and any restrictions based on such information, would run the risk of inhibiting the benefits that accrue to the United States from the free movement of technology. In light of these risks and the limited and uncertain nature of the potential benefits, we believe that significant monitoring and restriction of international technology transfer is both unworkable and unwise.

Chapter Three

COMPARISONS ACROSS AGENCIES

With the economic context as background, we now turn to federal agency policies for dealing with international technology transfers. This chapter first discusses how agencies view their tasking on international technology transfer within the broader context of their missions. It also addresses the issue of agency cooperation in fulfilling technology transfer functions. The chapter then describes and analyzes in detail the international technology transfer policies of the six agencies that account for the bulk of federal R&D: NASA, DoE, NIH, NIST's ATP within DoC, NSF, and DoD. Finally, it discusses policy implications.

OVERALL AGENCY STRUCTURE AND LAWS: A POTENTIAL CONFLICT

Agencies' goals arc initially set when the agency is created, either by legislation or, less usually, through an Executive Order. Over time, these goals change and usually increase as Congress or the President modifies them. Not surprisingly, federal agencies look to these explicit statements for guidance in executing their programs. As such, the basic goals of an agency are a powerful determinant of the activities of the agency. No agency has technology transfer as a basic goal.

To better understand agency goals and how they are interpreted, we collected a series of relevant documents. We started with the principal laws important to these agencies, such as the Space Act of 1958 for NASA. We also collected the most important laws dealing directly with technology transfer, such as the Federal Technology Transfer Act of 1986. Since many amendments have been made to these laws through the years, we also included the portions of the U.S. Code that incorporate most of these amendments. Finally, we reviewed the Code of Federal Regulations (CFR) for the implementation of these laws. This includes several better-known subsets of the CFR, such as the Defense Federal Acquisition Regulations and the DoE Acquisition Regulations (DEAR). The full CFR is enormous, but selected portions dealing with the matters discussed here are mentioned in the main discussion when they arise.

Each agency's dependence on its governing statute has an important effect. Specifically, there is a tendency to narrow goals that potentially conflict, so as to simplify decisions. We found that many agencies usually have only one dominant goal. Other goals are pursued only after the overall course of action is oriented by the primary goal. For example, NIH, discussed below, focuses on improving the health of the American people. Other goals, such as economic or social goals, are considered only *after* the overall goal has determined a course of action. In a sense, the other goals serve as constraints on the primary goal.

To examine this phenomenon, we also collected formal statements of goals for the agencies. Each statement is presented below in the treatment of the particular agency. The organization and behavior of each agency do indeed generally reflect its statement of goals.

One exception to this generalization appears when an agency is subdivided into several relatively autonomous suborganizations. In that case, individual offices may look to their particular founding legislation to provide their goals. This can be seen in DoC, for example, where the National Oceanic and Atmospheric Administration has a very different set of goals from NIST. In such cases, we believe that the individual suborganizations pursue their own primary goals. In this work, the only such suborganization we investigated in detail was the ATP within NIST.

This focus on a primary goal may seem to circumvent the intention of Congress or an administration in its direction to an agency. We do not find this to be the case. Rather, this focus reflects a reasonable response to the incommensurate goals often assigned to government agencies. To continue with the NIH example, improving the health of the American people is undoubtedly the primary reason the federal government appropriates funds to NIH. It is entirely reasonable for NIH to pursue other goals through its actions, such as economic prosperity for the American people, but few would argue that such other goals should take precedence over improving health.

And indeed, NIH pursues these other goals when they do not interfere with its primary goal. But when they do interfere, as when some discovery might have economic worth if owned by a firm but would have greater health benefits if available to all firms, foreign and domestic, the choice is to make the discovery available to all.

Agencies also organize in accordance with their primary goals. That is, the primary goal of an agency shapes the overall approach of the agency. Other, competing goals are addressed differently, usually separately. Overall, the goals of technology transfer are treated by the agencies we researched as a constraint on their activities in pursuit of other, primary goals.[1] One common approach we saw in technology transfer was the use of offices specifically charged with monitoring and promoting technology transfer. Such offices are also, sometimes, charged with monitoring the international flow of such technology. This behavior is hardly unique to technology transfer and is familiar from the response of agencies to many other laws, from equal opportunity to small business set-asides. At the same time, the rest of the agency organizes and focuses on the primary goal—health for NIH, space exploration for the space side of NASA, etc. We did not find an agency with noneconomic primary goals that attempted to embed the process of technology transfer within the general operations of the agency.

In most agencies, technology transfer has emphasized two often-related, but distinct, agency activities: the licensing of patents and the creation of various sorts of cooperative agreements. Both licenses and patents are relatively easy to count and to monitor. Not surprisingly, the same activities have been the primary focus of most of the legislative attempts to influence technology transfer. Our discussion of each agency naturally emphasizes these two activities as well.

This is in contrast to the much larger variety of mechanisms for technology transfer that are familiar from the economic literature and that are discussed in the first chapter of this report. In general, these other mechanisms emphasize the importance of person-to-person interaction in transferring technology. As developed in our discussion of the indicators of technology transfer below, this approach concentrates on the individuals involved in the cooperative agreements or the inventors of the patents. In general, however, details on the subsequent professional history of particular engineers or innovators are not available. In fact, in our interviews, many agencies expressed the belief that seeking such information would constitute an invasion of privacy. Other information on interpersonal contacts with foreigners, such as foreign visitors to a particular laboratory or participation at a meeting, appear of little utility here. Such data are *not* connected to the offices monitoring technology transfer and are not connected to particular innovations. This makes their interpretation unclear, even if the data were easily available.

In fact, others have noted the difficulty of gathering information here as well. A committee of the National Academy of Engineering writes, "meaningful data on the scope, growth, and nature of foreign institutions' involvement in publicly funded U.S. research is fragmentary, dated, and scarce." (Reid and Schriesheim, 1996b, p. 8.) Consequently, in our discussions of the federal

---

[1]An important exception to this is NIST's ATP. As we discuss below, the primary goal of ATP is in fact improving the performance of U.S. industry, so the goals of technology transfer (and of technology development) are central to the program. This is of course consistent with an agency emphasis on its primary goal.

agencies, we concentrated on the most available and least ambiguous indicators: foreign involvement in patents and in cooperative agreements.

Returning to the theme of how agencies cope with multiple goals, another approach to treating incommensurate goals is through an interagency process. The only example of such a process that we found involving technology transfer was the review for national security reasons of export licenses involving technology. There are actually two such formal processes, one for armaments through the Department of State, and one for "dual-use" exports through DoC. Both are coordinated and overseen by a formal, National Security Council–led interagency group. This is described below briefly when we discuss the DoD and more extensively elsewhere (NAS, 1991; Nolan et al., undated; and Agmon et al., 1996).

Two characteristics of this interagency process are important here. First, the emphasis of this process is on national security issues, not on issues of economics or the defense industrial base. Indeed, many audiences forcefully argue that only national security issues *should* be considered in this process (Nolan, et al., pp. 15ff). This is an interagency manifestation of a single goal dominating others—economic factors may be considered, but only at the margin, after the national security issues have determined the overall outcome.

Second, within this interagency process, each goal or set of goals is represented by a different agency. The traditional national security goals are represented by DoD;[2] diplomatic goals by the Department of State; economic goals by DoC; and arms limitation by the Arms Control and Disarmament Agency (ACDA).[3] This allows each agency to emphasize a single, primary goal internally. The role of the National Security Council oversight is to control the competition between these goals, elevating troublesome decisions until they are resolved. Importantly, it is *not* expected that individual agencies resolve such competing goals; rather, that is a role for the Executive Office of the President. The application of this interagency structure to issues involving international technology transfer is discussed in the final chapter of this document.

All these insights on technology transfer were gathered from conversations with individuals in six agencies who are involved with technology transfer. The six agencies were chosen to represent the primary federal agencies where the international transfer of technology developed with the assistance of the federal

---

[2]There are competing demands affecting technology transfer in the national security arena, but these are resolved within DoD; the department usually represents national security interests in the interagency process.

[3]Now that ACDA is integrated into the Department of State, it remains to be seen how clearly the latter viewpoint is expressed in this interagency process.

government seemed to us most at risk: NASA, DoE, NIH, NIST's ATP, NSF, and DoD.

These conversations were buttressed by collection of data on some methods of technology transfer. For most agencies, we aimed at the two major indicators of technology transfer that the agencies track: patents and cooperative agreements. For both patents and cooperative agreements, much information is available in principle. We asked if this information gave any indication of significant transfer of technology to foreign firms. In practice, both indicators proved to require significant additional effort to determine the relevant facts.

Specifically, we gathered data on U.S. patents that indicated support from any of three agencies—NASA, DoE, NIH—for selected years. This was to determine whether foreign entities or inventors were involved in patenting innovations with support from these agencies. We found that it was necessary both to gather data from the agency and to search the Patent and Trademark Office (PTO) database separately. Additionally, the search for foreign involvement was manual. The findings are reassuring though—in general, these agencies did not support significant foreign patenting. Those data are discussed below when we discuss each agency.

Additionally, we gathered data on the current status of the industrial participants in the ATP. This was designed to determine if companies involved in the ATP were being bought by foreign firms. Here, we found that many of the small firms involved in the ATP are privately held, and their fate after the expiration of the award proved time-consuming to determine. Again the findings were reassuring. In general, we found no evidence that these firms were being sold to foreign interests. These data will be discussed in more depth under the ATP discussion below.

We now turn to a discussion of each agency—its goals and how they are expressed and how it handles both cooperative agreements and the discrete bits of technology covered by patents and trade secrets.

NATIONAL AERONAUTICS AND SPACE ADMINISTRATION

Like most federal agencies, NASA looks to the statutes and executive orders that created it for its fundamental understanding of the goals and expectations the country has for it. The primary statute for NASA is the Space Act of 1958, which has since been much amended.

The Space Act and its history fairly reflect NASA's heritage, primarily growing out of the early space program with an emphasis on the peaceful exploitation of space. This heritage has shaped NASA's goals consistently; not surprisingly, the internal processes of the agency are designed to further those goals.

The following passage summarizes NASA's goals:

> The National Aeronautics and Space Administration conducts research for the solution of problems of flight within and outside the Earth's atmosphere and develops, constructs, tests, and operates aeronautical and space vehicles. It conducts activities required for the exploration of space with manned and unmanned vehicles and arranges for the most effective utilization of the scientific and engineering resources of the United States with other nations engaged in aeronautical and space activities for peaceful purposes. (National Archives, 1996, p. 583.)

The goals grow directly out of statute for NASA, as they do for most agencies. The amalgamated U.S. Code governing NASA does mention preserving the U.S. lead in space and aeronautics, but far down in a list. More importantly, it does not mention helping individual industrial firms or differentiating U.S. firms from others. The key passage reads,

> Objectives of aeronautical and space activities [of NASA]
> — Expansion of knowledge about the Earth and space
> — Improvements in air and space vehicles
> — Developing and using space vehicles
> — Long-range studies of the benefits and problems of the use of space
> — Preservation of a U.S. lead in related science and technology
> — Cooperation with the Department of Defense
> — International cooperation
> — Avoiding duplication within the United States
> — Preservation of the United States lead in aeronautics and space through research and technology development[4]

The internal representation of these goals are consistent with the general behavior of governmental agencies. NASA emphasizes its primary goal. For example, NASA states on its primary web page:

> When Congress created the National Aeronautics and Space Administration in 1958, it directed the NASA Administrator to do three things:
>
> 1. Conduct aeronautical and space "activities."
> 2. Create a science program using aeronautical and space vehicles.
> 3. Inform the public as widely as possible about agency activities and their benefits.[5]

Notably absent from the list is economic gain for the American people.

---

[4]Paraphrased from Title 42, Chapter 26—Nation Space Program, Subchapter I, from the National Aeronautics and Space Act of 1958, as amended.

[5]As accessed on November 13, 1996, at **http://www.gsfc.nasa.gov/hqpao/hqpao_home.html**

Historically, NASA actually has two distinct sources with differing perspectives and policies. One source is NASA's heritage from the National Advisory Committee on Aeronautics (NACA), which existed from its founding in 1915 until its inclusion in NASA in 1958 (Mowery and Rosenberg, 1982, p. 101). The aeronautics part of NASA still maintains a relationship with the U.S. aircraft industry and sees its role as aiding that industry. The larger, space exploration side of NASA emphasizes the first task above and draws its heritage from the Apollo program, planetary exploration, and now the International Space Station. This part of NASA emphasizes international cooperation, which has always been a major factor in the civilian U.S. space program.

In both parts of NASA, one underlying principle governs the creation of new technologies. Fundamentally, new technologies are justified for a mission of the agency; commercial value is a secondary, but positive benefit. This is true not only for the technologies created in NASA's centers by federal employees, but also for the technologies created in most Space Act agreements as well.

Space Act agreements are the cooperative R&D form most commonly used at NASA. They are allowed by the Space Act (thus the name), and include more latitude for NASA than do the Federal Technology Transfer Act amendments to Stevenson-Wydler. Specifically, under a Space Act agreement, NASA can fund the activities of a private firm, something impossible under the government-wide authority of the Federal Technology Transfer Act.[6]

For NASA, technology transfer concerns two activities—the disposition of discrete pieces of intellectual property involving the agency and creating these cooperative agreements. This intellectual property can be in two forms. The most familiar is patents, and there are established procedures at NASA for handling and licensing them. The other form is a potential "trade secret," and NASA does not have the legislative authority actually to create such intellectual property. In practice, intellectual property created at NASA that fits this category has little protection at NASA.[7]

Organizationally, the control over these discrete bits of intellectual property and over the Space Act agreements is primarily internal to NASA. Both are usually structured in ways that promote U.S. firms. The intellectual property includes both patents and the trade secrets owned by firms, but known to NASA. Policy for these is generally centered in the Office of the General Counsel. A notable exception to this internal control involves patents. Patent control is delegated to universities when applicable, in accordance with Bayh-

---

[6]This authority arises from the "Administration" title of the Space Act.

[7]This does *not* apply to trade secrets revealed to NASA by other entities. Authority for protecting such intellectual property is in place at NASA.

Dole (P.L. 96-517) and its extension by President Reagan, contained in Office of Management and Budget (OMB) Circular A-124, and thus is external. Additionally, a great deal of attention is paid to safeguarding trade secrets owned by firms.

A largely unrelated aspect of international technology transfer at NASA concerns export controls for national security reasons. These are the controls administered by the Department of State under the International Traffic in Arms Regulations and those administered by DoC under the Export Administration Regulations. Both of these limitations are discussed in more depth in our discussion of the DoD, where they are a dominant concern. All agencies of the government must work within the framework of these laws. NASA is somewhat more affected than other agencies, both because of the nature of the technology it uses and because of the importance of international cooperation to the space part of NASA.

Within NASA, the procedures for dealing with both of these national security–related controls are well-described (NASA, 1997a). Not surprisingly, given that export regulation is hardly a central goal of NASA, these demands are met by a network of special offices concerned just with these regulations. These start with an office at NASA Headquarters, called the Headquarters Export Administrator, and involve a network of Center Export Administrators at each field center (NASA, 1997a, p. 2-3).

There is a single emphasis in the presentations that NASA makes to its staff on these limitations: Do not ignore these limits. The presumption is that the scientists and engineers within NASA are most often surprised to learn of these limitations, which interfere with their desires to export equipment to various international partners. There is utterly no discussion of other reasons to limit such exports, only a discussion of how to use the NASA offices to meet the demand of the sets of regulations (NASA, 1997b).

For cooperative agreements and for both patents and trade secrets, there is no evidence of interagency coordination on policy or practice. This is in contrast to the established interagency procedures for both the International Traffic in Arms Regulations and the Export Administration Regulations. Those procedures are also described in more detail in our chapter on DoD.

Patents

For patents, NASA has a well-established system. Now government-wide under Public Law 96-517, Section 209, this procedure for dealing with federally owned patents originated in NASA:

- Patents are first published in the Federal Register.

- Anyone interested in licensing the patent files a description of the plans, including those for commercialization.

- If the application is to "use or sell in the U.S." the plan must normally be that "any products . . . will be substantially manufactured in the U.S."

Public Law 96-517 is the 1980 amendment to the Patent and Trademark law. Its restrictions now apply to all licenses of federally owned patents. The key term, *substantially*, is not defined and so is up to the discretion of individual agencies. This law does not rule out licenses to foreign firms, as long as the manufacturing follows the last criterion above. In practice, NASA does license patents to foreign companies and feels that it *must* under some treaty agreements that the United States has.

Overall, NASA is involved with three classes of patents:

- those derived from a cooperative agreement and owned by the private entity involved

- those derived from a cooperative agreement and owned by NASA

- those derived from NASA research with no outside partner.

Even in the first case, when the patent is owned by the private entity, the last of the three government-wide licensing restrictions still applies through language in the cooperative agreement. In general, when a cooperative agreement is involved, the patenting procedure depends on whether the private partner wishes to own the innovation. If the private entity wishes to own the patent, NASA must grant a waiver allowing this, which it almost always does. In keeping with the Bayh-Dole Act and the extension under OMB Circular A-124, the government retains a royalty-free license[8] and march-in rights, which allow the U.S. government to revoke a license if the private license holder is not bringing the innovation to market.[9] If the entity is not interested, NASA may patent the innovation on its own. The entity retains a royalty-free license. When researchers at NASA produce a patentable innovation separate from any cooperative agreement, NASA simply owns the patent outright. These patents are then available for licensing.

Findings on Patenting

One potential method of technology transfer to foreign interests can be checked through an inspection of patents. If a government agency supports the research leading to a U.S. patent, that information should be reflected in the

---

[8]35 U.S. Code 202(c) (4).

[9]35 U.S. Code 203.

information on that patent in the PTO database. Additionally, each agency is required to monitor the patents it owns, as well as the patents created through various cooperative agreements. The lists of patents from such monitoring can be a check on the PTO database. If such patents are being created by foreigners or are being assigned to foreign entities, that would be an indication that foreign technology transfer is occurring in these programs.

In the case of NASA, we investigated all patents that showed a connection to NASA and were granted in 1992, in 1995, and in 1996–1997. We chose 1992 because, by then, most of the laws influencing technology transfer had been enacted, yet it was sufficiently long ago that the monitoring and reporting system, which is based on self-reporting, should have had time to assemble the data. The latter years were included to indicate current trends at NASA.

For 1992, we eventually assembled a list of 235 patents, either reported by NASA or found in the PTO database under a search for "NASA." Figure 3.1 shows the distribution of these patents broken out into various categories. NASA's internal records contained 192 patents. Of those, we had found 178 in the search for "NASA" in the PTO database. The remaining 14 we had not found showed no mention of NASA in the PTO database. Additionally, we found five patents assigned to NASA in the PTO database, but not on NASA's internal list, and 40 patents (including two of the five just mentioned) that had a declared "NASA interest" in the PTO database but not in NASA's. The distribution for the later years is qualitatively similar.

The omission of some patents from NASA's internal database surprised us. That database consists of anything reported to NASA centers through New Technology Reports from a contractor, which are required under contract, or through invention disclosures from employees. The NASA centers then report that information to NASA headquarters, where it gets entered into the TechTrek system. The system then tracks those inventions and, if patents are granted for those inventions, lists the patent numbers. There are several potential reasons the PTO database would list NASA as the assignee, even though NASA does not have the patent in its internal records:

1. NASA is the assignee, but does not have the patent listed in its database. Not all NASA centers are up to date on their reporting information.

2. NASA is not the assignee, but the PTO database lists NASA as the assignee. The PTO will sometimes list the name or organization that is on the front of the patent, rather than the actual assignee, which is listed in the document.

The reason is *not* that the PTO database does not keep track of reassignments of patents. NASA does not reassign any of its patents to other entities, so reassignment would not be a cause for the gaps between the PTO database and NASA's TechTrek System.

RAND*MR979-3.1*

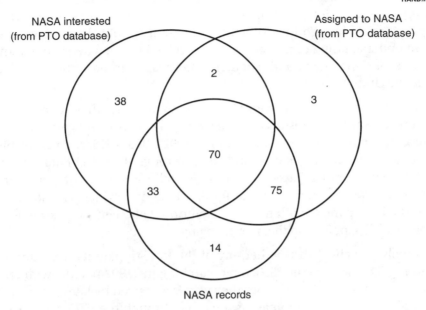

Figure 3.1—1992 Patents Related to NASA

We believe that NASA's internal database, TechTrek, simply has no driving need to be comprehensive. The information on the patents is apparently only used for general indicators of NASA's activity. As such, the large subset in the internal database is probably sufficient. For our purposes, we looked at the entire set of patents for each year.

We searched all of these patents for indications of foreign involvement. Foreign involvement could mean either that the patent had one or more inventors from outside the United States or that the patent was assigned to a foreign national or a foreign company (or both). Note that there is an important caveat for the foreign inventors: By law, foreign nationals residing in the United States for more than one year are not required to list their citizenship on a patent application. This may have skewed our results for reporting foreign inventors, but not for foreign assignees.

Our attention to foreign inventors is an imperfect measure of international technology transfer. We searched for this because foreign inventors will automatically carry an understanding of the technology in the patent back to their country, if and when they leave the United States. A foreign inventor thus can be an indirect measure of technology transfer through personnel movement. On the other hand, this does not affect ownership of the patent. Consequently, NASA can enforce the appropriate licensing restrictions for the use of the patent within the United States. Furthermore, the involvement of foreign nationals or even foreign assignees can also be an entirely positive indication that NASA is pursuing another of its goals noted above: international cooperation. The full interpretation of foreign involvement in a patent should thus involve a sub-stantive understanding of the technology involved in the patent, to determine both its economic worth and whether NASA was tapping unusual expertise outside the United States.

For our concerns with international technology transfer, these complications seem unnecessary. The results of our search showed little indication of signifi-cant foreign involvement. For our sample—1992, 1995, 1996, and part of 1997—707 NASA-related patents were found either through the NASA database or the PTO database. Among those, we found a total of nine patents with foreign inventors labeled as such and one foreign assignee, which is also counted among the nine patents with foreign inventors. This seems an extremely low number, with no indication that it is changing.

Additionally, we checked whether any of the foreign patents were unusually influential. This was accomplished by searching the 1992 patents with foreign involvement to determine whether they were referenced by later patents. This is a simple form of citation analysis, possible through the PTO database. We chose only the 1992 patents because the later years have not had time to show up as references, given the usual delay in patent citations. The results are shown in Table 3.1.

The table shows that the foreign-related patents from 1992 are all cited by other patents. To understand whether this is unusual, the most obvious comparison would be with the set of all NASA-related patents from 1992, perhaps differenti-ated by technical area. For a quick impression, we checked for citations to eight other patents. Of those eight, two had no citations, three had one, one had three, one had four, and one had eight citations. Qualitatively, this is a similar distribution. Given the very small numbers of these patents, we did not investi-gate them further. And again, since the ownership of all these patents resides domestically, any financial benefits should be captured domestically.

Overall, this investigation of patents showed that there was little obvious for-eign involvement in U.S. patents related to NASA. This is not surprising. How-ever, it is not the whole story, even for patents. This entire search concerned only U.S. patents. That was a natural focus, as most of the laws restricting patents deal only with the use of federal technology for use or sale within the United States, and thus only concern U.S. patents. The international transfer of these technologies might well be indicated by patents involving the same tech-nology elsewhere.

We have no information on whether these patents have been filed elsewhere. More importantly, we have not looked at similar patents in other nations, so the

Table 3.1

Citations to 1992 NASA Patents with Foreign Involvement

Patent Number	Title	Relation to NASA	Foreign Involvement	Source of Patent	Referenced by Patents
5,085,252	Method of forming variable cross-sectional shaped three-dimensional fabrics	Government interest	Foreign inventor	PTO database	5,465,760 5,435,352 5,404,917 5,224,519
5,118,781	Poly(1,3,4-oxadiozoles) via aromatic nucleophilic displacement	Assigned to NASA	Foreign inventor	PTO and NASA databases	5,626,406
5,123,017	Remote maintenance monitoring system	Assigned to NASA and government interest	Foreign inventor	PTO and NASA databases	5,642,478 5,600,788 5,590,395 5,581,482 5,572,670 5,553,237 5,550,751 5,528,752 5,491,791 5,388,252 5,357,427 5,305,235
5,130,990	VLSI architecture for a Reed-Solomon decoder	Assigned to NASA and government interest	Foreign inventor	PTO and NASA databases	5,517,509 5,444,719 5,373,511 5,329,535 5,323,402

possibility remains that foreign entities are patenting NASA-derived technologies elsewhere after they are revealed in a U.S. patent. More complex foreign behaviors are also possible, such as restricting the applicability of a foreign filing by filing other patents that "surround" its applicability. An investigation of such behaviors and their implications for the international transfer of technology was beyond our resources.

Trade Secrets

We now return to our discussion of NASA's overall management of the other aspects of technology transfer. Trade secrets are another category of discrete intellectual property but are quite different from patents. The key is that NASA does not have the authority to protect trade secrets that it creates outside of a Space Act agreement. This seems to be a particular problem for the aeronautical part of NASA. Such potential trade secrets are evidently easy for NASA to identify internally. Unfortunately for those wishing to protect such information, NASA interprets the Freedom of Information Act and the Space Act to mean that NASA must publish potential trade secrets openly. These potential trade secrets are discrete items, such as computer codes for aircraft design. NASA is not allowed even to copyright the government software.

This procedure is consistent with the legacy of NACA, which published its information openly. During much of NACA's history, the U.S. aeronautical industry dominated the world, so that the exploitation of published data was largely by U.S. firms. Open publication thus allowed NACA not to show favoritism among firms. Today, the primary competitors to U.S. firms are overseas, and thus open publication can end up aiding competitors to U.S. firms.

NASA would like to change this situation, so that it can safeguard and then transmit to U.S. firms any trade secrets it creates. The new Espionage Law,[10] which defines a trade secret, does not negate the perceived requirement on NASA to publish. Without changing the requirement to publish, NASA cannot take advantage of the Espionage Law because it cannot restrict knowledge of such an innovation. In the opinion of NASA's counsels, changing the requirement to publish requires a change to the Space Act. This has been proposed in several NASA authorization bills and included in them, but those bills have never been enacted into law. Consequently, this is a continuing problem for NASA.

Cooperative Agreements

NASA also has an established procedure for cooperative agreements under the Space Act. These can be structured to ensure that benefits accrue to U.S. companies, and often are. Larger cooperative agreements, initiated by NASA when the agency feels it has something of value, are advertised in the Federal Register as a Cooperative Agreement Notice. In many large cases, as for the X-33 and the X-34, the administrator of NASA rules that only U.S. companies are eligible; in general, the competitions are open. Since the purpose of a cooperative agreement is to stimulate or support a public purpose, these are normally only won by domestic firms. Public comments are invited. Smaller cooperative agreements are often at the instigation of a private firm. In those cases, NASA has no obligation to open the competition or to ask for comments, and it rarely does so.

The detailed procedures for these cooperative agreements are codified in the CFR, 14 CFR Part 1274. Those regulations describe how NASA is to administer and fund Space Act cooperative agreements in great detail.

---

[10]The Economic Espionage Act of 1996: Public Law 104-294; 18 USC 1831-1839.

DEPARTMENT OF ENERGY

More so than many of the other agencies we discuss here, the DoE has a complex institutional history. This complexity still effects both the organization of the department and its sense of mission.

Organizationally, the department can trace some of its roots to the Atomic Energy Commission (AEC), established in 1946. AEC was created to provide civilian control for the development of the nuclear weaponry of the DoD. It also found itself with the responsibility for the development, promotion, and regulation of commercial nuclear power. Some basic research was also included in this mix, most famously for high-energy physics. The mission of the agency was broadened in response to the energy crises of the 1970s to encompass a multitude of energy programs, from conservation to coal. These programs, which came from agencies as diverse as NSF, the Interior Department, and the Environmental Protection Agency, all had their own roots, some of which predated AEC. In almost all cases, these predecessor programs had been conceived of in isolation. That is, the problems were seen as problems of "coal" or of "automobile efficiency," rather than as parts of an integrated energy problem. The energy crisis changed that and allowed the creation of a single agency bridging these different areas. Institutionally, there were a parallel set of changes, culminating in the formation of DoE in 1977 (Fehner and Holl,1997).

Both of the original two nuclear roles continue to influence DoE, although the Nuclear Regulatory Agency, created by the Energy Reorganization Act of 1974, has taken over the regulatory role. The elements of other agencies that were drawn into the DoE also maintain their heritage and roles and thus influence DoE as well.

These different roles are fundamentally based upon the legislative authority that underlies DoE. The department's legacy of isolated problems is still reflected in the diversity of those governing statutes, which have originated in differing committees of Congress. Thus, for example, restrictions on foreign participation in R&D programs imposed by the 1992 Energy Policy Act, similar to those of the ATP, do not apply to high-energy physics and coal research.[11]

These divergent roles are reflected in the statements of the goals of DoE. The following is one such statement:

> The Department of Energy, in partnership with its customers, is entrusted to contribute to the welfare of the Nation by providing the technical information and the scientific and educational foundation for the technology, policy, and institutional leadership necessary to achieve efficiency in energy use, diversity

---

[11]Code of Federal Regulation, Title 10—Energy, Chapter I—Department of Energy, Part 600—Financial Assistance Rules, Subpart F—Eligibility Determination for Certain Financial Assistance Program—General Statement of Policy, September 2, 1997.

in energy sources, a more productive and competitive economy, improved environmental quality, and a secure national defense. (National Archives, 1996.)

Economic benefits are included, but only as one of five goals that the activities of the department—the "technical information and the scientific and educational foundation [relevant to energy]"—are intended to support.

Additionally, the complexity of these differing laws has generated a complex set of regulations in the CFR: the DEAR. These regulations include the language mentioned above on foreign participation in R&D programs, as well as the description of patent rights, waivers (for government ownership of patents), and the large number of other details necessary for government contracts. Generally, in the code, nuclear energy is covered in the U.S. Code, Title 423, Chapter 23. This includes sections on R&D (Section 2051) and on patents (Section 2181). Non-nuclear energy is governed by Title 42, Chapter 74, which has corresponding sections on the federal programs that are permissible in the pursuit of the goals, such as contracting for research (5906) and on patents (5908).

Laboratories

An important set of institutions for technology within DoE are its laboratories, which have significant autonomy. Historically, the national laboratories have not had technology transfer as their primary goal. In a pattern similar to that of other agencies, technology transfer is often the responsibility of an office within each laboratory. That office is responsible for implementing the policies and procedures defined in DEAR. Almost all of them have a corresponding web site. Table 3.2 simply lists the Universal Resource Locators (URLs) for those sites:

These web sites differ but, in general, provide a connection to the office that is concerned with technology transfer at the individual laboratory. These offices then lead any viewer to overviews of licensing, cooperative agreements, etc. The emphasis is typically on the advantages of working with the laboratory in question; limitations are dealt with in passing. For example, from the discussion of cooperative agreements at the Lawrence Livermore web site, there is only a mention of the limitations we are looking at: "[An agreement] Requires technical collaboration by the industrial partner. Usually accompanied by a license or option agreement. Requires 'substantial U.S. manufacture' of resulting products or services."[12] Even the "substantial U.S. manufacture" phrase is

---

[12]As accessed on November 28, 1997: **http://www.llnl.gov/IPandC/ipc-home/crada.html**

Table 3.2

DoE URLs for Technology Transfer Policies

Laboratory	Home Page	Technology Transfer Page
Argonne National Laboratory (ANL)	http://www.anl.gov/	http://www.itd.anl.gov/
Brookhaven National Laboratory (BNL)	http://www.bnl.gov/ bnl.html	http://www.bnl.gov/TECHXFER/ tech_transfer.html
Fermi National Accelerator Lab (Fermilab)	http://www.fnal.gov/	
Idaho National Engineering Laboratory (INEEL)	http://www.inel.gov/	
Lawrence Berkeley Laboratory (LBL)	http://www.lbl.gov/	http://www.lbl.gov/Tech-Transfer/ index.html
Lawrence Livermore National Laboratory (LLNL)	http://www.llnl.gov/	http://www.llnl.gov/IPandC/ IPandC.shtml
Los Alamos National Laboratory (LANL)	http://www.lanl.gov/	http://www.lanl.gov/Internal/ projects/IPO/wrk_wIPO.html
National Renewable Energy Laboratory (NREL)	http://www.nrel.gov/	http://www.nrel.gov/documents/ plan/5.html
Oak Ridge National Laboratory (ORNL)	http://www.ornl.gov/	http://www.ornl.gov/patent/ ornl_ott.html
Pacific Northwest National Laboratory (PNNL)	http://www.pnl.gov:2080/	http://www.pnl.gov/partner.html
Sandia National Laboratory (SNL)	http://www.ca.sandia.gov	http://www.ca.sandia.gov/Tt.html
Stanford Linear Accelerator Center (SLAC)	http://www.slac.stanford. edu	http://www.slac.stanford.edu/ grp/irm/techtransfer/techtransfer .html

missing from the web page on licensing.[13] A similar pattern can be found at Sandia National Laboratory, with only the web page for cooperative agreements mentioning the "substantial U.S. manufacturing" requirement.[14] We expect these examples are ordinary simplifications, adopted to make the web site readable rather than comprehensive.

While we did not investigate the individual laboratories in depth, one laboratory did reply to our requests for specific information on their technology transfer controls: Lawrence Livermore National Laboratory (LLNL). LLNL's deputy director has reported that "we are very concerned about licensing to foreign companies and are thus very cautious and conservative." (Kiefer, 1997.) Nonetheless, he went on to state that "LLNL has written policies and procedures on technology transfer, but not specifically on technology transfer to for-

---

[13]As accessed on November 28, 1997: **http://www.llnl.gov/IPandC/ipc-home/license.html**

[14]As accessed on November 28, 1997: **http://www.ca.sandia.gov/casite/sbi.html**

eign nationals or foreign companies." (Kiefer, 1997.) They then note that the policies on licensing and cooperative agreements do give preference to U.S. companies. In general though, Lawrence Livermore National Laboratory "uses the technology transfer policies, procedures, and directives of the Department of Energy and other federal laws and directives. . . ." Finally, they note that Livermore has licensed technologies to foreign firms and has some cooperative agreements in place with such firms, but that such efforts are few compared with the much larger number of efforts with U.S. firms (Kiefer, 1997).

Additionally, the laboratories are the one place in DoE where trade secret–type intellectual property might be created by the government. Such trade secrets are simply the property of the contractor running the laboratory, usually for a limited time of five years. Consequently, government disclosure is not an issue, as the government does not know of the trade secret.

Overall, we are left with an impression that the DoE laboratories are simply executing the policies in place at higher organizational levels. We did not further check the actual practices of the laboratories, however.

Cooperative Agreements

Cooperative agreements are seen as an important part of technology transfer at DoE, particularly for the large laboratories. Implicitly, the international transfer of technology within the agreements is controlled through regulations on the initial access to the program. The general metaphor is one of a "level playing field"—that is, a situation where U.S. firms would have equivalent access to programs in the other nation.

The rules are explicitly patterned after the ATP rules. In formulation, the rules were coordinated with the Departments of State, Commerce, and the Treasury, and with the Executive Office of the President. In implementation, we are aware of no ongoing interagency coordination.

The language has interesting differences from the ATP rules, discussed below. On foreign participation in cooperative agreements, the DoE-approved language says that

> The Parties [to a cooperative agreement, or CRADA] agree that a purpose of this CRADA is to provide substantial benefit to the U.S. economy.
>
> In exchange for the benefits received under this CRADA, the Participant therefore agrees to the following:
>
> A. Products embodying Intellectual Property developed under this CRADA shall be substantially manufactured in the United States;
>
> B. Processes, services, and improvements thereof which are covered by Intellectual Property developed under this CRADA shall be incorporated into the Par-

ticipant's manufacturing facilities in the United States either prior to or simultaneously with implementation outside the United States. Such processes, services, and improvements, when implemented outside the U.S., shall not result in reduction of the use of the same processes, services, or improvements in the United States; and

C. The Contractor [running the laboratory as a Government-Owned, Contractor-Operated facility] agrees to a U.S. Industrial Competitiveness clause in accordance with its prime contract with respect to any licensing or assignment of its intellectual property rights arising from this CRADA, except that any licensing or assignment of its intellectual property rights to the Participant shall be in accordance with the terms of Paragraphs A. and B. of this Article.[15]

Several of these requirements, such as the requirement for simultaneous implementation here and abroad, have no parallel in the ATP rules.

For cooperative agreements, DoE must also enforce the government-wide requirements for the "level playing field." There are problematic countries that cause DoE the most difficulty in reaching decisions. These are countries where the issue of U.S. access to the equivalent programs is debatable. Israel and Japan were the two mentioned to us in conversations as currently being problematic. Additionally, and in spite of the eventual ruling, a waiver can be sought to allow foreign participation in a cooperative agreement. DoE has granted waivers allowing Japanese participation, in particular.

There is no interagency coordination of these determinations involving DoE. We are also not aware of any interagency coordination for another set of determinations, unique to DoE. These are the determinations of "foreign ownership, control, or influence" over a contractor, which are invoked when the contractor might have access to either classified information or a "significant quantity of special nuclear material, as defined in 10 CFR Part 710."[16] Both of these situations are in contrast to the established interagency process involving national security controls on exports, which is even embedded in the standard DoE cooperative agreement.[17] We discuss that process under the DoD.

Patents

Patents are a focus of the technology transfer activities within DoE. While trade secrets are dealt with in passing, primarily at the laboratories, licensing of patents is one focus of the DoE laboratories, in particular. In general, the DoE applies the same rules and regulations as NASA in licensing decisions.

---

[15]*Article XXII, DOE-Approved CRADA Language,* **http://www.doe.gov/techtran/crdshrt.html**, as accessed on August 14, 1997.

[16]DEAR, Section 952.204-73.

[17]*Article XXII, DOE-Approved CRADA Language,* **http://www.doe.gov/techtran/crdshrt.html**, as accessed on August 14, 1997.

The Bayh-Dole Act (Public Law 96-517) forms the basis across the agency. The ownership of the patent is thus vested in the private entity if one is involved. The familiar requirement for manufacture to be "substantially" in the United States for sale here is maintained. Additionally, these requirements are usually extended for the results of contract research done for DoE.

One problem in these controls on the international transfer of technologies was raised in our conversations with DoE. Specifically, the Office of the General Counsel expressed a concern that the intent behind the Bayh-Dole Act was being circumvented. That law restricts the "licensing" of patents, requiring that any exploitation of the patent for sale or use within the United States be performed "substantially" within the United States. This is an attempt to capture the economic gains of the patent for the nation.

The law does not mention explicitly the assignment of a patent, however. An assignment would occur when a company is sold and assigns (not licenses) its patents to the buying firm. For many of the institutions covered by the Bayh-Dole Act, this is not relevant. A university is not going to be "sold" in the ordinary course of business and so does not have the opportunity to assign its patents. The potential arises for other categories of company, such as small businesses, which are indeed often sold, and for larger firms, which may become involved under the extensions of the Bayh-Dole Act.

In fact, the patent counsels within DoE had two such instances involving a small business. In the first case, in the words of the DoE representative,

> Arco-Solar received millions of dollars of DOE funding over several years because the DOE program was trying to make a U.S. company the world leader in photovoltaics. We then learned that Siemens was planning to purchase Arco-Solar. We tried to block the sale through a proceeding before the Treasury Department but were unsuccessful. (Hightower, 1997.)

In the second case,

> In 1991 Los Alamos National Laboratory (LANL) granted an exclusive license to Cell Robotics [that] was bought out by Micel, Inc., a Delaware corporation, which was wholly owned by Mitsui Engineering and Shipbuilding (MES), a Japanese company. We found out about the sale from the Department of State. LANL had failed to put a U.S. manufacture requirement in the license (required by Bayh-Dole) but we were able to get LANL to amend the license to require the U.S. manufacture to requirement. (Hightower, 1997.)

These are the only two such cases we know of. The economic importance of these two patents is undoubtedly small on the scale of the U.S. economy. In a gross economic sense then, there is no compelling reason to make a change. On the other hand, it would appear that this loophole in the Bayh-Dole Law could be removed by a simple insertion of "or assignment" to the U.S. Code. We return to this point in our summary observations, at the end of this report.

Findings on Patenting

As we discussed above under NASA, one potential method of technology transfer to foreign interests can be checked through an inspection of patents. If a government agency supports the research leading to a U.S. patent, that information should be reflected in the information on that patent in the PTO database. Additionally, each agency is required to monitor the patents it owns, as well as the patents created through various cooperative agreements. The lists of patents from such monitoring can be a check on the PTO database. If such patents are being created by foreigners or are being assigned to foreign entities, that would be an indication that foreign technology transfer is occurring in these programs.

In the case of DoE, we investigated all patents that showed a connection to DoE and that were granted in 1992, in 1995, and in 1996–1997. We chose 1992 because, by then, most of the laws influencing technology transfer had been enacted, yet it was long-enough ago that the monitoring and reporting system, which are based on self-reporting, should have had time to assemble the data. The latter years were included to indicate current trends at DoE.

For 1992, we eventually assembled a list of 474 patents, either reported by DoE or found in the PTO database under a search for "DoE" or related terms. Figure 3.2 shows the distribution of these patents broken out into various categories. DoE's internal records contained 372 patents. Of those, we had found 339 in the search for "DoE" in the PTO database. The remaining 33 we had not found showed no mention of DoE in the PTO database. Additionally, we found four patents assigned to DoE in the PTO database, but not on DoE's internal list, and 101 patents (including three of the four just mentioned) that had a declared "DoE interest" in the PTO database but that were not in the DoE database. Once DoE assigns a patent, it no longer tracks it, which may account for some of these missing patents. The distribution for the later years is qualitatively similar.

Like NASA's, DoE's internal database omits some patents. We have no detailed knowledge of the internal workings of DoE's database. Just as with NASA, there are several potential reasons the PTO database would list DoE as the assignee, but DoE would not have the patent in their internal records:

1. DoE is the assignee but does not have the patent listed in its database because of some failure in reporting from a lower bureaucratic level.

2. DoE is not the assignee, but the PTO database lists DoE as the assignee. The PTO will sometimes list the name or organization that is on the front of the patent, rather than the actual assignee, which is listed in the document.

RAND*MR979-3.2*

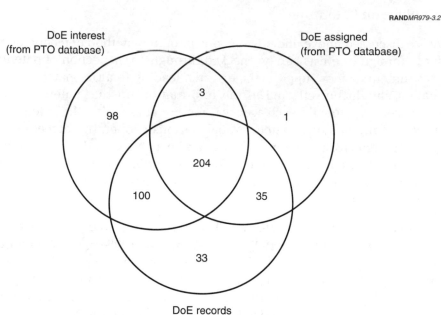

Figure 3.2—1992 Patents Related to DoE

As in the case of NASA, DoE's internal database does not need to be comprehensive. The information on the patents is apparently only used for general indicators of DoE's activity. As such, the large subset in the internal database is probably sufficient. For our purposes, we looked at all the patents for each year.

We then searched all of these patents for indications of foreign involvement. Foreign involvement could mean either that the patent had one or more inventors from outside the United States or that the patent was assigned to a foreign national or a foreign company (or both). Note that there is an important caveat for the foreign inventors: By law, foreign nationals residing in the United States for more than one year are not required to list their citizenship on a patent application. This may have skewed our results for reporting foreign inventors but not for foreign assignees.

Our attention to foreign inventors is an imperfect measure of international technology transfer. We searched for this because foreign inventors will automatically carry an understanding of the technology in the patent back to their country, if and when they leave the United States. A foreign inventor thus can be an indirect measure of technology transfer through personnel movement. On the other hand, this does not affect ownership of the patent. Consequently, DoE can enforce the appropriate licensing restrictions for the use of the patent within the United States. Furthermore, the involvement of foreign nationals or even foreign assignees can also be an entirely positive indication that DoE is tapping foreign expertise needed domestically. The full interpretation of foreign involvement in a patent should thus involve a substantive understanding of the technology involved in the patent, to determine both its economic worth and whether DoE was tapping unusual expertise outside the United States.

For our concerns with international technology transfer, these complications seem unnecessary. The results of our search showed little indication of significant foreign involvement. For our sample—1992, 1995, 1996, and part of 1997—1,498 DoE-related patents were found either through the DoE database or the PTO database. Among those, we found a total of 33 patents with foreign inventors labeled as such, as well as nine foreign assignees. Seven of the foreign assigned patents also were counted among the patents with foreign inventors. The nine foreign assignees are shown in Table 3.3. In all cases, the DoE had an interest in but no claim on the patent, and the patent was found by our search of the PTO database. None of the patents below was found in the DoE database.

Both the number of foreign inventors and the number of foreign-assigned patents are low in comparison with the total number of patents involving DoE. The changes over time are more noticeable than for NASA, however. The num-

Table 3.3

DoE Patents with Foreign Assignments

Patent Number	Title	Foreign Involvement
RE34,819	Gold-nickel-titanium brazing alloy (reissue of patent #4,938,922 originally issued July 3, 1990)	Foreign assignee
5,439,578	Multiple capillary biochemical analyzer	Both foreign inventor and foreign assignee
5,443,806	Treating exhaust gas from a pressurized fluidized bed reaction system	Both foreign inventor and foreign assignee
5,571,639	Computer-aided engineering system for design of sequence arrays and lithographic masks	Foreign assignee
5,491,967	Pressurized fluidized bed reactor and a method of operating the same	Both foreign inventor and foreign assignee
5,499,498	Pressurized fluidized bed reactor	Both foreign inventor and foreign assignee
5,526,582	Pressurized reactor system and a method of operating the same	Both foreign inventor and foreign assignee
5,567,294	Multiple capillary biochemical analyzer with barrier member	Both foreign inventor and foreign assignee
5,583,081	Copper-containing zeolite catalysts	Both foreign inventor and foreign assignee

ber of patents with foreign inventors remained consistently small for all the years we investigated. The number of foreign assignees did increase, from zero in 1992 to six in 1996–1997 (the bottom six in Table 3.3). With such small numbers, it might be that DoE has simply taken advantage of particular foreign expertise to further these fields. Alternatively, this might indicate a trend of more foreign support from DoE. Without a substantive analysis of the six patents, however, these alternatives cannot be distinguished.

Additionally, we checked whether any of the foreign patents were of unusual influence. This was accomplished by searching the 1992 patents with foreign involvement to determine whether they were referenced by later patents. This is a simple form of citation analysis, possible through the PTO database. We chose only the 1992 patents, as the later years have not had time to show up as references, given the usual delay in patent citations. The results are shown in Table 3.4.

Table 3.4 shows that seven of the nine foreign-related patents from 1992 are cited by subsequent patents.[18] To understand whether this is unusual, the most obvious comparison would be with the set of all DoE-related patents from 1992, perhaps differentiated by technical area. For a quick impression, we checked for citations to the 18 patents above and below these nine in our complete list. Of those 18, five had no citations; five had one; one had two; one had three; two had four; two had five; one had seven; and one had eight citations. Qualitatively, this distribution is similar to that in the table. Given the very small numbers of these patents, we did not investigate them further. Also, and as the above data show, there were no foreign assigned patents in 1992. Again, since the ownership of all these patents resides domestically, any financial benefits should be captured domestically.

Overall, this investigation showed little obvious foreign involvement in U.S. patents related to DoE. It is important to recall that this search concerned only U.S. patents. That was a natural focus, as most of the laws restricting patents deal only with the use of federal technology for use or sale within the United States, and thus only concern U.S. patents. The international transfer of these technologies might well be indicated by patents involving the same technology elsewhere.

We have no information on whether these patents have been filed elsewhere and have not looked at similar patents in other nations, so the possibility remains that foreign entities are patenting DoE-derived technologies elsewhere after they are revealed in a U.S. patent. More complex foreign behaviors are

---

[18]Note that indeed two of the patents have the same name, although their numbers differ.

Table 3.4

Patents from 1992 with DoE Involvement and a Foreign Inventor—Citations

Title	DoE Involvement	Source of Information	Referenced By
Composite membranes for fluid separations	DoE interest	DoE and PTO database	5,601,769 5,342,432 5,286,280 5,222,388
Compositions containing poly (.gamma.-glut-amylcysteinyl)glycines	DoE has both interest in and holds patent	DoE and PTO database	None
Cyclohexyl-triethylenetetraamine hexacetic acid	DoE interest	DoE and PTO database	5,635,157 5,476,644 5,428,156 5,292,938
Optical switching system and method	DoE not mentioned	DoE only	5,305,123
Ceramic materials with low thermal conductivity and low coefficients of thermal expansion	DoE interest	PTO database	5,433,778 5,322,559 5,268,199
Kit for the selective labeling of red blood cells in whole blood with .sup.9 TC	DoE interest	DoE and PTO database	None
Boron containing compounds and their preparation and use in neutron capture therapy	DoE has both interest in and holds patent	DoE and PTO database	5,545,397 5,492,900 5,455,022 5,280,119 5,171,849
Boron containing compounds and their preparation and use in neutron capture therapy	DoE has both interest in and holds patent	DoE and PTO database	5,630,786 5,492,900 5,455,022
Magnetostrictive resonance excitation	Assigned to DoE	DoE and PTO database	5,641,905 5,533,399

also possible, such as restricting the applicability of a foreign filing by filing other patents that "surround" its applicability. An investigation of such behaviors and their implications for the international transfer of technology was beyond our resources.

NATIONAL INSTITUTES OF HEALTH

NIH is formally part of the Public Health System (PHS) in the Department of Health and Human Services (HHS). Despite this relatively low bureaucratic position, NIH has significant autonomy and a healthy budget, both due to its solid political support. That support is motivated by the simple appeal of the goal of NIH:

> The institute seeks to expand fundamental knowledge about the nature and behavior of living systems, to apply that knowledge to extend the health of human lives, and to reduce the burdens resulting from disease and disability. It supports biomedical and behavioral research domestically and abroad, conducts research in its own laboratories and clinics, trains promising young researchers, and promotes, acquiring and distributing medical knowledge. (National Archives, 1996, pp. 286–267.)

The importance of improving the health of the American populace is clearly both a lasting and an important goal. Even more importantly, it is one that is transparently clear to the voters and, thus, to their representatives. This is well-reflected in the pertinent passages from the U.S. Code:

> The Director of NIH shall—
>
> (2) coordinate, review, and facilitate the systematic identification and evaluation of clinically relevant information from research conducted by or through the national research institutes;
>
> (3) promote the effective transfer of the information described in paragraph (2) to the health care community and to entities that require such information . . . .[19]

Not surprisingly, the law says nothing distinguishing U.S. firms or entities from foreign ones; the criterion is only health benefits. This is in keeping with the pattern we have seen in other agencies, where the primary goal is dominant, and other goals are treated as constraints on achieving the primary goal.

Also in keeping with this pattern, NIH contains an Office of Technology Transfer to oversee transfers from NIH to other entities of all sorts. This office sets policy on technology transfer for the entire PHS and executes the policy for all but the Centers for Disease Control. The office is thus key to NIH's policies and actions. Its activities seem primarily to concern controls over patents, and our analyses concentrated there.

Patents

Technology transfer for the Office of Technology Transfer at NIH primarily concerns patenting and the licensing of patents. The office also oversees technologies that are simply transferred by two other routes. One of these other routes is when NIH manufactures and sells some material itself. These are pri-

---

[19]Title 42, Section 282(e), or The Public Health Service Act of 1944, as amended.

marily research materials, not clinical ones. Additionally, this course is followed when the cost of duplicating the material outside of NIH is high. In such cases, simply supplying the materials "at cost" is a natural extension of the research ethos that characterizes NIH.

Another unusual route is a straightforward publication of a method. The notional example cited to us was a tablet coating that could be applied to many medications. Publication, so that all firms may use the method, is chosen when that is the best way to make the health benefits of a method available to the public. It is chosen *even if the methods are commercially important.* Again, this choice is clearly correct in pursuit of the goal of improving health.

Patents are still important for NIH and often used. Patents are necessary whenever a technology available for transfer requires a large investment to become a useful innovation. NIH prefers nonexclusive licenses, so as to increase the availability of some innovation for improving health. That is not always feasible, however. For NIH, the obvious example of this is a typical new drug. The costs of the required trials to establish safety and efficacy are such that a company wishing to commercialize almost any new drug will require an exclusive license.

The procedures that NIH follows for licensing a patent are well-defined. They seem generally designed to assure openness and fairness in the licensing process, while getting the patentable developments to the public as quickly as possible. First, NIH will advertise any available patents or patentable discoveries widely. When multiple firms wish to license the patent, NIH will chose a firm based on ability to commercialize. As noted, exclusive licenses are granted if commercialization costs are high, although NIH tries to involve multiple companies if there are multiple applications. Finally, if multiple firms are equally likely to commercialize the innovation, the Bayh-Dole Act (P.L. 96-517) and its extension by President Reagan, contained in OMB Circular A-124, and the Federal Technology Transfer Act constraints are applied. As is explicit in this listing, however, these constraints are only reached when all else is equal. If all else is *not* equal, such as if a U.S. firm is considered less able to commercialize a patent, the patent is granted to a firm that can, regardless of ownership.

Such patenting usually involves only United States patents. International patents are sometimes sought, but only when the company involved with the commercialization has a strong interest in such patents. NIH, on its own, will rarely file for international patents.

NIH carefully monitors its licensees to make sure that they are proceeding to commercialize their licenses. A failure to commercialize a license, as might in principle occur if a new drug promised to reduce the income from some older, more established drug, triggers action to revoke a license and to find a new licensee. Again, this is directly related to the interest in getting a patent through to commercialization, so that it can help the American people; it is not related to the ownership of the firm commercializing the innovation.

Technology transfer policy is treated by the NIH as an internal matter. It does not consult with interagency groups for technology transfer policy or for decisionmaking on particular transfers. Informal contacts, particularly with DoC, are available, through the Federal Laboratory Consortium and the Technology Transfer Working Group. These were described to us as opportunities for voluntary information sharing and networking only.

Findings on Patenting

Unlike NASA and DoE, NIH was unable to provide us a list of its patents. Consequently, we relied exclusively on the PTO database for this investigation. Judging by the results for DoE and NASA, we assume this sample to be incomplete but representative of the total population. As with the other agencies, we investigated all patents that showed a connection to NIH and that were granted in 1992, in 1995, and in 1996–1997.

A complication of this analysis is that NIH exists within a larger hierarchy. As noted, NIH is part of the PHS, which is in turn part of the HHS. Given our experience, we expected all of those agency names to show up on some patents that originated within NIH. Of course, other parts of the PHS, such as the Centers for Disease Control, would also produce patents cited as PHS or HHS; similarly, other parts of HHS could produce patents simply cited as HHS. We checked the influence of these other agency names by searching for patents under their names as well. Interestingly, the number of patents citing HHS and especially the PHS are smaller than those simply citing NIH, presumably indicating the importance of NIH in creating such intellectual property. In Table 3.5, we have not corrected the categories for the double-counting that occurs when a patent lists more than one term, such as NIH *and* HHS, but have simply included the patents in both categories.

We then searched all of these patents for indications of foreign involvement. Foreign involvement could mean either that the patent had one or more inventors from outside the United States or that the patent was assigned to a foreign national or a foreign company (or both). Note that there is an important caveat for the foreign inventors: By law, foreign nationals residing in the United States for more than one year are not required to list their citizenship on a patent application. This may have skewed our results for reporting foreign inventors, but not for foreign assignees.

Our attention to foreign inventors is not a perfect measure of international technology transfer. Foreign inventors carry an understanding of the technology in the patent back to their country, if and when they leave the United

Table 3.5

Foreign Involvement in Patents at NIH

Agency	Year	Total Patents	Foreign Inventors Number	Foreign Inventors Percentage	Foreign Assignments Number	Foreign Assignments Percentage
NIH	1992	126	8	6.3	2	1.6
	1995	264	24	9.1	0	0.0
	1996–97	738	81	11.0	12	1.6
HHS	1992	105	14	13.3	4	3.8
	1995	115	17	14.8	2	1.8
	1996–97	277	36	13.0	3	1.1
PHS	1992	16	2	12.5	0	0.0
	1995	19	1	5.3	1	5.3
	1996–97	38	6	15.8	0	0.0

States. A foreign inventor thus can be an indirect measure of technology transfer through personnel movement. On the other hand, this does not effect ownership of the patent. Consequently, NIH can enforce the appropriate licensing ogy in the patent back to their country, if and when they leave the United restrictions for the use of the patent within the United States. Furthermore, the involvement of foreign nationals or even foreign assignees can also be an entirely positive indication that NIH is pursuing another of its goals noted above: supporting biomedical and behavioral research abroad. The full interpretation of foreign involvement in a patent should thus involve a substantive understanding of the technology involved in the patent, to determine whether NIH was tapping or developing unusual expertise outside the United States.

The results of our search showed a moderate indication of foreign involvement. For our sample—1992, 1995, 1996, and part of 1997—1,681 distinct patents were found in the PTO database under NIH, PHS, or HHS. Table 3.5 totals 1,698, because we have not corrected for the 19 patents that cite two agency names. Of the patents in the table with foreign involvement, only two in 1992 and three in 1996 and 1997 with foreign inventors are double counted; none of the foreign-assigned patents are double counted. Among the members of this set, we found a total of 184 patents with foreign inventors labeled as such (corrected for the double counting just noted) and 24 with foreign assignees. In some cases, the foreign assignee shares the assignment with a private U.S. entity or even with the federal agency listed. In many cases, but not all, the patents with foreign assignments also had foreign inventors. The overall distribution across the agency names and years is shown in Table 3.5.

In contrast to our results for NASA and DoE, these results show a significant contribution from foreign inventors. Approximately 10 percent of the patents associated with these activities over time have involved foreign inventors. The percentage may also be growing slightly over this period, but our data are

insufficient to determine that. In contrast, the patents assigned to foreign entities are a fluctuating, but small percentage.

Assessing the importance of this foreign involvement is difficult. As with NASA
and DoE, we attempted to determine the importance by searching the 1992
patents with foreign involvement to determine whether they were referenced
by later patents. This is a simple form of citation analysis, possible through the
PTO database. We chose only the 1992 patents, because the later years have not
had time to show up as references, given the usual delay in patent citations.
The results are shown in Table 3.6. As the table shows, there is a familiar distribution in the number of citations. We did not prepare a comparison specifically for this set of patents, but the numbers and distribution of citations are
similar to those we noted for DoE and NASA. A more detailed examination of
this comparison, differentiating by technology, would be useful, as it would also
be for the DoE and NASA patents.

Besides the uncertainties concerning the importance of these patents, other
caveats also apply, as they did for the NASA and DoE analyses. This entire
search concerned only U.S. patents. That was a natural focus, as most of the
laws restricting patents deal only with the use of federal technology for use or
sale within the United States and thus concern only U.S. patents. The international transfer of these technologies might well be indicated by patents involving the same technology elsewhere.

We have no information on whether these patents have been filed elsewhere.
Neither have we looked at similar patents in other nations, so the possibility
remains that foreign entities are patenting these technologies elsewhere after
they are revealed in a U.S. patent. More complex foreign behaviors are also
possible, such as restricting the applicability of a foreign filing by filing other
patents that "surround" its applicability. An investigation of such behaviors
and their implications for the international transfer of technology was beyond
our resources but would be interesting.

ADVANCED TECHNOLOGY PROGRAM

Our investigation of NIST has focused on ATP, because of its prominence.
Unlike all the other agencies we investigated, NIST has a clear focus on economic effects. It states its goal as:

> The National Institute of Standards and Technology (NIST) assists industry in
> developing technology to improve product quality, modernize manufacturing
> processes, ensure product reliability, and facilitate rapid commercialization of
> products based on new scientific discoveries.

Table 3.6

Citations to NIH-Related Patents from 1992

Patent Number	Title	Foreign Code	Referenced By
5,173,481	Preparation of specifically substituted cyclodextrins	I	5,608,015
5,171,750	Substituted phenserines as specific inhibitors of acetyl-cholinesterase	I	5,639,892 5,621,114 5,550,254 5,550,253 5,547,977 5,541,340 5,541,216 5,523,442 5,480,651 5,409,948
5,173,292	Monoclonal antibodies that specifically recognize galacto-syl-globoside, compositions containing same and methods of using same	I	None
5,145,962	Human pro relaxin polypeptides	B	None
5,122,468	Hut-78 cell lines infected with HTLV-III that secrete gp160	A	5,447,837
5,116,740	Method for producing native HIV gp160	A	5,554,499 5,254,457
5,114,942	Treating habit disorders	I	None
5,169,521	Apparatus for countercurrent chromatography separations	I	5,547,580 5,496,741 5,449,461
5,135,864	Rapid, versatile and simple system for expressing genes in eukaryotic cells	B	5,597,896 5,565,319
5,132,212	SCL gene, and a hematopoietic growth and differentiation factor encoded thereby	I	5,650,317 5,214,133
5,123,201	Sensor-triggered suction trap for collecting gravid mosquitoes	I	None
5,116,867	D-propranolol as a selective adenosine antagonist	I	None
5,104,531	Cross-axis synchronous flow through coil planet centrifuge for large-scale preparative countercurrent chromatography	I	5,380,429
5,096,893	Regioselective substitutions in cyclodextrins	I	5,633,368 5,608,015
5,092,885	Peptides with laminin activity	I	5,567,408 5,556,609 5,548,062 5,500,013 5,330,911 5,278,063
5,078,553	Compact drill sampler for quantitation of microorganisms in wood	I	5,437,368 5,256,012

Table 3.6—Continued

Patent Number	Title	Foreign Code	Referenced By
5,143,753	Suppression of electroosmosis with hydrolytically stable coatings	I	5,415,747
5,080,771	Capillary gels formed by spatially progressive polymerization using migrating initiator	I	5,453,163
5,175,292	Intermediates for the preparation of dideoxycarbocyclic nucleosides	I	5,631,370
5,173,292	Monoclonal antibodies which specifically recognize galacto-syl-globoside, compositions containing same and methods of using same	I	None
5,171,667	Hybridomas producing monoclonal antibodies to mono-, di- and trifucosylated type 2 chain	I	None
5,149,543	Ionically cross-linked polymeric microcapsules	I	5,654,006
			5,650,116
			5,573,934
			5,562,909
			5,562,893
			5,562,099
			5,548,060
			5,543,158
			5,529,914
			5,529,777
			5,500,161
			5,494,673
			5,487,390
			5,464,932
			5,290,765
			5,286,495
5,130,538	Method of producing multiply charged ions and for deter-mining molecular weights of molecules by use of the mul-tiply charged ions of molecules	I	5,581,080
			5,567,938
			5,470,753
			5,440,119
			5,376,789
			5,300,771
			5,352,891
			5,298,744
5,126,494	Methods for catalytic asymmetric dihydroxylation of olefins	I	5,491,237
			5,420,366
			5,419,817
			5,302,257
			5,260,461
5,106,969	Biologically active thiazine	B	None
5,092,391	Device for the continuous casting of thin metal products between rolls	B	None

NOTE: I = foreign inventor, A = foreign assignee, B = both foreign inventor and foreign assignee.

> The Institute's primary mission is to promote U.S. economic growth by working with industry to develop and apply technology, measurements, and standards. (National Archives, 1996, p. 165.)

This emphasis is, if anything, even more pronounced in the ATP, which traces its goals to the Omnibus Trade and Competitiveness Act of 1988, as amended by the American Technology Preeminence Act of 1991. These acts define the purpose of the ATP to be assisting U.S. business to commercialize new discoveries rapidly and to refine manufacturing technologies. Explicitly, they say the purpose is "improving the competitive position of the United States and its businesses . . . ."[20]

The ATP focuses on cooperative agreements. These are essentially the only activity within it and are the aspect we concentrated on. Licensing of patents would only occur if the government exercised its march-in rights and gained ownership of a valuable patent. To our knowledge, that has not yet happened.

The statutes define several important aspects of the cooperative agreements at the core of the ATP. Foreign participation is limited. The laws restrict access to the program to "a United States–owned company . . ." or to subsidiaries of other companies, if the home company's country allows access to similar programs for U.S. firms.[21] Additionally, the laws require "monitoring how technologies developed in [the program's] research program are used, and reporting annually to the Congress on the extent of any overseas transfer of these technologies."[22]

With such a clear statement, the economic goals of the ATP dominate other goals. For this program, these goals are the primary ones, and others are subordinate. Not surprisingly, the policies and the regulations of the ATP center on processes for achieving these goals. For example, there is no office of technology transfer within the ATP; rather, that is the purpose of the entire program. Moreover, the entirety of the ATP consists of federal-private agreements, so the aspects of technology transfer that are similar to those governing eligibility to cooperative agreements, predominate.

The regulations are part of the CFR. 15 CFR Part 295 is the ATP rule. These regulations simply implement the language in the statutes above.

The limitation on foreign ownership appears in the regulations as:

---

[20]US Code 15 Section 278n, subsection (a).

[21]US Code 15 Section 278n, subsection (d), (9), (B).

[22]US Code 15 Section 278n, subsection (c), (2).

(a) A company shall be eligible to receive an award from the Program only if:

(1) The Program finds that the company's participation in the Program would be in the economic interest of the United States, as evidenced by investments in the United States in research, development, and manufacturing (including, for example, the manufacture of major components or subassemblies in the United States); significant contributions to employment in the United States; and agreement with respect to any technology arising from assistance provided by the Program to promote the manufacture within the United States of products resulting from that technology (taking into account the goals of promoting the competitiveness of United States industry), and to procure parts and materials from competitive suppliers; and

(2) Either the company is a United States–owned company, or the Program finds that the company is incorporated in the United States and has a parent company which is incorporated in a country which affords to United States–owned companies opportunities, comparable to those afforded to any other company, to participate in any joint venture similar to those authorized under the Program; affords the United States–owned companies local investment opportunities comparable to those afforded to any other company; and affords adequate and effective protection for the intellectual property rights of United States–owned companies.

(b) The Program may, within 30 days after notice to Congress, suspend a company or joint venture from continued assistance under the Program if the Program determines that the company, the country of incorporation of the company or a parent company, or the joint venture has failed to satisfy any of the criteria contained in paragraph (a) of this section, and that it is in the national interest of the United States to do so.[23]

Furthermore, those same rules define a foreign firm as:

(r) The term "United States–owned company" means a for-profit organization, including sole proprietors, partnerships, or corporations, that has a majority ownership or control by individuals who are citizens of the United States.[24]

Note part (b) above, which allows the ATP to suspend an award if the status of a company changes. This is typical of the additional detail gained when going from code to regulations; the agency is attempting to extend the intent of Congress to a particular case that was not explicitly considered in the writing of the law. Here, the extension seems quite straightforward and uncomplicated.

Determining eligibility is only the first step for an ATP award. The determination forms an initial screen that a proposal must pass before consideration by

---

[23]Sec. 295.2 Eligibility of United States– and Foreign-Owned Businesses, as accessed on August 15, 1997, at **http://www.atp.nist.gov/atp/kit/atprule.htm** .

[24]Sec. 295.2 Eligibility of United States– and Foreign-Owned Businesses, as accessed on August 15, 1997, at **http://www.atp.nist.gov/atp/kit/atprule.htm** .

both a technical and a business panel. These panels explicitly must weigh the potential economic gain, as well as the technical feasibility of the proposal.

In all, three formal "screens" try to capture and control the economic benefits for the United States:

- requirements for entry, as described
- reviews during the course of an award
- post-award monitoring period.

Finally, some firms also wish to win future awards, which informally will depend upon any past experience with the firm in the program.

The reviews during the course of an award are of three types:

- quarterly reports on progress, with particular attention to technical and business mileposts
- annual site visits
- telephone conversations and other communications, as necessary.

These monitoring methods allow the ATP office to make sure an agreement is being implemented as planned, including the location of research and production in the United States. The office also monitors the continuing ownership of the participants and the involvement of key individuals.

These reviews are supplemented by a different set of reviews after the conclusion of an award. The ATP requires firms to take part in an evaluation period after the end of the agreement for the intellectual property developed under the program, including the involvement of that intellectual property in

- licensing
- joint ventures
- strategic alliances
- outright sales.

As is implicit in the above, the ownership of the intellectual property developed within the ATP is with the private entities, not with the government. Additionally, and as is common when the United States grants title to intellectual property developed with the help of the government, the government retains march-in rights, which would be used if a participant were not actively pursuing a market.

The after-agreement monitoring, defined to be six years, is not as strongly enforceable as the monitoring during an agreement. Consequently, the ATP office attempts to keep the demands on the firms low for this monitoring. Additionally, several aspects of technology transfer, such as the location of the key individuals involved in the research, cannot in fact be monitored at all after the conclusion of the agreement. So far, the firms have been quite willing to participate in this monitoring, but only a comparatively few ATP efforts have reached this stage. The style and method of this monitoring is now being reexamined by the ATP. Additionally, the Economic Assessment Office within the ATP intends to estimate the full societal benefits of the ATP agreements, at least for the United States. This is an ambitious undertaking, and that office is investigating several methods of making this assessment.

Interagency Coordination

Essentially all the controls exercised over the ATP are imposed and monitored through DoC and, in fact, through NIST. No formal interagency process is involved, although informal contacts do exist between DoC and other agencies. These informal contacts exist for two reasons. The ATP program has two mandates that require some interaction with other agencies. Both are irregular, in that they are triggered by individual applications, and not by some regularly scheduled review cycle.

First, ATP is required to avoid "unnecessary duplication" of research activities. They accomplish this avoidance through informal communications with other R&D agencies of the federal government.

Second, whenever a foreign-owned firm is a substantive partner in a proposal, the ATP office must make a "finding" to allow that firm to participate. This finding is in accordance with the ATP Eligibility Rules, as described above. Basically, the finding has three features outside the proposal substance. One feature is that "any equivalent programs" in the nation of ownership of the parent firm be open to U.S.-owned firms. The second feature is that the nation in question protect intellectual property rights. The third feature is that opportunities are afforded in the other nation for local investment by U.S. firms. To check these aspects, the program office contacts the U.S. trade representative, the State Department, and other agencies, as appropriate.

Neither of these processes is a formal interagency process. While the ATP is aware of similar findings, as by parts of the DoE, there is no explicit sharing of results or analyses between the agencies.

As noted above, NIST and the ATP office are required to report on the use of the technologies developed in the program and on any overseas transfer of these technologies. To date, these reports have been simple and of relatively low visibility. Fundamentally, this is because the ATP is still a young program. Only a few of the ATP efforts have had the time to reach market—thus, describing their use is a short task. Likewise, the ATP has seen little evidence of foreign transfers of technology developed within the program.

Analysis of the ATP Awardees

The eligibility screens for foreign ownership within the ATP seem quite robust. Still, the government has not been able to control the technologies developed within the program fully after a particular award has been completed; beyond the reporting period, the company has no obligation to report on the disposition of the technology, and the individuals involved have no restrictions on their activities.

Some methods of the international transfer of the technology can be tracked, however. In particular, the ownership of the private entities can be tracked, at least in principle. We know from the DoE example that transfers of ownership of a private firm can be a method of international transfer of technology. We checked on this by tracking the ownership of companies that had received early ATP awards. We focused on the early awards because those awards have (mostly) been completed by now, and moreover, the firms involved have had an opportunity to be bought and sold in the years since the award.

We examined all ATP general awards from 1990 through 1994, a total of 121 awards. We gathered the names of all entities participating in these awards, a total of 339 separate entities. In the cases of academic institutions, industry consortia, and government entities, this identification information was sufficient to identify whether the entity was a U.S. entity. In the case we are most concerned with, of company participants, identification was less clear. To identify company participants, we used the OneSource database. OneSource, Inc., is "a leading provider of business and financial information" on public and private companies. Although OneSource charges a fee for use of its data, we were able to gain access to OneSource through a public library at DoC. In most cases, we were able to procure the desired company information using OneSource. In a few cases, additional research through other sources was needed to identify changes in ownership or name that occurred after the ATP award.

Most of the companies were clearly identified. Of the 339 participating entities, we were unable to identify the national affiliation of only 36 companies. Four of these 36 companies are identified as subsidiaries of private parents whose ultimate ownership is not available. The remaining 32 companies are not found in the OneSource database.

Many of the companies were also clearly domestic. However, the limitations of the databases forced us to make some assumptions. In particular, we assumed that nonsubsidiary private companies with headquarters in the United States are U.S. companies. Information on the actual ownership of such companies is not generally available.

Table 3.7 contains the most important summary data obtained from our search. In general, foreign participation in these ATP general awards was quite limited. Of 339 entities participating in 1990–1994 general awards, we identified only six foreign entities—one foreign university and five foreign companies.

The foreign university was the University of Montreal, for award 91-01-0224, entitled "Development and Applications of Density Functional Software for Chemical and Biomolecular Modelings."[25] The fact that this was a foreign university was certainly obvious to the ATP program. In this award, it was teamed with a U.S. firm, Biosym Technologies, Inc., of San Diego, California.

The five foreign-owned firms are similar, in that they were all divisions of well-known foreign firms: one division from Royal Dutch Petroleum and two each from Philips Electronics and British Petroleum. In four cases, they were teamed with U.S. firms. The one exception without a U.S. firm involvement is award 93-01-0045 to Philips Laboratories, entitled "A Novel Microminiature Light Source Technology."

Several conclusions emerge from these results. First, the hurdles for foreign participation in the ATP have resulted in little explicit foreign involvement. Second, there are *no* observed cases of foreign purchase of involved firms. While we did find some instances of firms having been bought since their award, there was no evidence of foreign involvement in those sales. The important caveats to this are (1) the unknown companies, whose ownership remains

Table 3.7

Summary of ATP Awards

	1990	1991	1992	1993	1994	Total
Total Awards	11	28	29	21	32	121
Participating Entities	41	108	44	75	71	339
Companies	34	81	33	63	61	272
U.S. Owned	32	71	24	54	50	231
Foreign Owned	0	0	0	1	4	5
Unknown	2	10	9	8	7	36

---

[25]The first two digits of the award code indicate the year, in this case, 1991.

unclear, and (2) the ownership of privately held firms, which we assumed was identical to their headquarters location. While foreign involvement remains possible given these uncertainties, we have no evidence to support that possibility. It would thus appear that the ATP has largely succeeded in restricting the involvement of foreign countries.

NATIONAL SCIENCE FOUNDATION

NSF's governing statute is the National Science Foundation Act of 1950, as amended. It currently enumerates seven goals for the agency.

> The Foundation is authorized and directed—
> (1) to initiate and support basic scientific research and programs to strengthen scientific research potential and science education programs . . . and to initiate and support research fundamental to the engineering process and programs to strengthen engineering research potential and engineering education programs . . .
> (2) to award . . . scholarships and graduate fellowships . . .
> (3) to foster the interchange of . . . information . . . in the United States and foreign countries
> (4) to . . . support the development . . . of methods and technologies, primarily for research and education
> (5) to evaluate the status and needs of the various . . . fields
> (6) to provide a central clearinghouse for the collection, interpretation, and analysis of data on science and engineering resources
> (7) to . . . maintain a program for the determination of the total amount of money for scientific an engineering research . . . received by each educational institution and non-profit organization in the United States.[26]

Notably absent from this list is the promotion of the U.S. economy or of the capability of individual firms. Rather, the goals all cluster around the creation and diffusion of knowledge.

These goals are faithfully reproduced in the agency's renditions of its own goals. As one example states:

> The National Science Foundation promotes the progress of science and engineering through the support of research and education programs. Its major emphasis is on high-quality, merit-selected research—the search for improved understanding of the fundamental laws of nature upon which our future well-being as a nation depends. Its educational programs are aimed at ensuring increased understanding of science and engineering at all educational levels, maintaining an adequate supply of scientists, engineers, and science educators to meet our country's needs. (National Archives, 1996, p. 617.)

---

[26]National Science Foundation Act of 1950, as amended (42 USC 1861-1875).

NSF follows a variation on the pattern we have seen in other agencies in which economic benefits are not a central goal. Technology transfer is interpreted narrowly as a matter of patents and licensing. Also in keeping with the pattern, the policy for and oversight of patents and licensing at NSF are the responsibility of a specific office within the agency. For NSF, that is the office of the General Counsel, where there is an Associate General Counsel specifically for patents and intellectual property rights. This office makes sure the agency follows the applicable laws and federal regulations. For example, the agency maintains a nonexclusive license for the federal government for any patent,[27] and also maintains march-in rights, exercisable primarily if commercialization of the patent is not being pursued.[28]

Since NSF has no laboratories or other facilities, cooperative agreements are irrelevant to its operation. Quite in contrast to the ATP, patent licensing is NSF's primary concern involving technology transfer.

Patents

The handling of patents at the NSF is unusual because of the extensive delegation of responsibility to their grantees. Unlike NASA or NIH, it has no laboratories staffed by government employees and, unlike DoE, no large, contractor-run facilities. The vast majority of the grantees of NSF are universities or other nonprofits. Consequently, essentially all of NSF's grantees fall under the Bayh-Dole Act (Public Law 96-517) or its extension by President Reagan, contained in OMB Circular A-124. The NSF delegates the enforcement of the constraints of the Bayh-Dole Act to its grantees. Moreover, the agency has no oversight of that enforcement.

There has in fact been an explicit decision at the agency level *not* to collect information on disposition of patent rights. With the advent of the Government Performance and Results Act, though, this policy has recently been questioned internally at NSF. Clearly, information on the number and use of patents might help indicate the worth of NSF's research. At the same time, the gathering and analysis of the information would entail costs.

Trade Secrets

Potential trade secrets are another category of intellectual property that can be created through NSF grants. Currently, the agency has a policy of disclosing any information submitted to it as a result of research. This is seen as impor-

---

[27]35 U.S. Code 202(c) (4).

[28]35 U.S. Code 203.

tant to the general principle that information discovered through NSF's grants is for the good of the general public. In practice, NSF has no choice but to allow a grantee not to disclose some finding, if the grantee so chooses. This avoids disclosure, since if the information is transferred to NSF, it is open to all. Certainly, it cannot be protected at NSF as a potential trade secret must be.

Nondisclosure, since it is at odds with the general philosophy at NSF, is tacitly discouraged. Nonetheless, some trade secrets have apparently been developed with NSF funding (at least in part). Such cases are rare and are handled individually; so far, no serious dispute has arisen. The agency knows few details of any such trade secret.

Other Methods of Technology Transfer

NSF is aware of the many other ways that technologies can be transferred, quite apart from the discrete pieces that might be embedded in a patent or a trade secret. In fact, much of the research on such methods was funded by the Social, Behavioral and Economic Sciences Directorate of NSF. Nonetheless, the agency does not seek to limit such transfers and does not track them for information on international (or other) technology transfer.

One such method of international technology transfer, perhaps the most important, is the movement of trained personnel overseas. NSF has highly aggregated information on foreign graduate students. However, it has no detailed tracking that connects particular grants and such students and does not track those students' subsequent status (as resident aliens, return to country of origin, etc.). Other personnel contacts, such as with visitors or at conferences, are not regularly reported. In fact, NSF has no policies limiting such contacts. Such rules would obstruct one goal listed above, "to foster the interchange of . . . information . . . in the United States and foreign countries," which may account for their absence.

DEPARTMENT OF DEFENSE

Unlike the other agencies we have discussed, the DoD has quite explicit, high-level guidance, codified in national strategy documents signed by the President. These documents are updated periodically, as required by the Goldwater-Nichols Defense Department Reorganization Act of 1986. The documents enumerate DoD's ultimate goals and the strategy for attaining them. As such, they serve as the guide for most departmental decisions.

At the highest level, the "central goals" of the National Security Strategy are simple and basic. In their latest incarnation, they are

> To sustain our security with military forces that are ready to fight.

To bolster America's economic revitalization.

To promote democracy abroad. (White House, 1995, p. i.)

Technology immediately becomes involved with these strategies, as technological superiority is essential to the military strategy that supports the National Security Strategy. The military strategy identifies a need to maintain technological superiority in U.S. weaponry to defeat enemies. It also identifies a need to maintain interoperability with potential allies and coalition partners. Finally, the strategy recognizes that our allies should have superior weaponry as well so that they may play an effective role in coalition with us. Indeed, technological collaboration is important to the NATO alliance in particular, in which perceptions of U.S. reluctance to share advanced technologies cause friction.

Maintaining technological superiority is pursued along two basic tracks. First, DoD invests in new technologies and weapons, primarily through private firms. For DoD, the issue of technology transfer is often dominated by questions of weapon sales; transfers of technologies by themselves are relatively rare. Technologies are most commonly transferred in connection with the sale of a weapon system.

Second, the international transfers of those technologies are limited, to maintain a U.S. advantage. The tension between this last point and the need to transfer systems to our allies is obvious. To adjudicate this tension, the United States uses an interagency process, coordinated by the National Security Council.

This interagency process is the only significant one we found among the agencies examined. Our treatment of DoD concentrates on that process, to the exclusion of the patenting and cooperative agreement policies we examine for the other agencies. This is so that the applicability of a new, similar interagency process involving the economic aspects of the international transfer of technology can be better assessed.

The legal basis for restricting exports of technologies rests upon two laws: the Arms Export Control Act, under which the Department of State administers the International Transfer in Arms Regulations (ITAR), and the Export Administration Act,[29] under which DoC has the authority to control and restrict *all* exports from the United States. The ITAR lists all weapons and related items whose international sales are restricted. Technology restrictions are applied to "dual-use" items that contain technologies useful in both civilian and military products. These restrictions are codified in the Commodity Control List (CCL).

---

[29]As continued under the International Emergency Economic Powers Act, 50 U.S.C. 1703(b). The Export Administration Act itself expired on August 20, 1994, but its provisions have been carried forward by a succession of Executive Orders since then, using the authority of the above act.

Penalties exist for those exporting in violation of these laws and their related regulations. Internationally, these restrictions were coordinated through the Coordinating Committee for Multilateral Export Controls prior to the end of the Soviet Union. Since the collapse of the communist system, some controls have been continued under the coordination of the new Wassenaar Arrangement. This history has been described more fully elsewhere and does not directly concern our subject (NAS, 1991; Nolan et al., undated; Agmon et al., 1996).

For the purposes of this document, the key point is that these restrictions were intended to limit the military capability of other nations—the traditional "national security" objective. Indeed, many influential commentators argue that this general issue should be the *only* one weighed when transfers of arms or related technology are at issue. As the recent Presidential Advisory Board states,

> The fundamental principles of national security, international and regional security, and arms control must be the basis for international agreement. The inevitable economic pressures that will confront individual states should not be allowed to subvert these principles. (Nolan et al., undated, p. 26.)

Economic rationales, either for or against a sale, are distinctly secondary factors and are perhaps not relevant to these commentators. Even commentators willing to consider economic effects in potential transfers of technology still recognize the very large role of the more traditional national security interests in decisions (NAS, 1991, pp. 107f).

Most of the arguments on economic factors involve the *positive* economic reasons to allow a sale. The debate does not usually consider restrictions motivated by national economic gain. Such debates do occur though; the most memorable recent debate was that involving the FS-X program with Japan. In that case, the concern was that the transfer of technologies from the F-16 program would help the Japanese develop a commercial aircraft industry (Lorell, 1995, especially Chapters Eight and Nine). Similar debates have occurred over other license requests, but they remain much the exception.

National policy is consistent with the broad outlines of these arguments. Presidential Decision Directive Number 34, Conventional Arms Transfer Policy, places economic objectives secondary to national military objectives. There is an implication that if there are no negative national military implications of a transfer, economic effects may be considered in making the decision. Implicitly, the economic effects would *favor* the sale.

The identification of the technologies to be restricted remains a major issue, both nationally and internationally. Nationally, the DoD created and maintains the Military Critical Technologies List to provide a listing of items the department is concerned about transferring without further scrutiny. This serves as an input to the ITAR list of weapons and related items maintained and administered by the Department of State and the CCL of dual-use technologies maintained and administered by DoC. Deciding under which list certain technologies should be controlled remains a contentious issue because the CCL regulations are seen as less constraining than those administered under the ITAR. Recent examples that have involved the interagency process extensively have been communication satellites and computer encryption software. In both those cases, the pressure from industry was to move the items from the ITAR to the CCL, to ease sales abroad.

The export control process itself is managed through the exchange of export license documents among agencies involved (at a minimum, the departments of State, Defense, and Commerce) and among intelligence agencies and offices. Internally to the DoD, there is also a relatively elaborate coordination process. The actual flow of documents is a major problem to those monitoring applications for licenses as well as those monitoring the aftereffects. Lack of a common database and of historical files is reflected in the lack of uniformity on decisions and implementation.

Several agencies maintain investigative activities to report on the use of exports. These include most notably the departments of State and Commerce, and the Federal Bureau of Investigation. Additionally, the intelligence agencies provide much information, although they are still adjusting to the need to assess allies' and U.S. technologies. Defense attachés and liaison officers also provide information. Generally, all of these agencies are behind in their capabilities— both in assessing what we should protect and in assessing how others might use what they are given.

Most export license decisions are made by category of item and category of end user. These are naturally specific to a given technology and country. Dual-use technologies regulated by Commerce are categorized by technology and by recipient, with different categories of recipient allowed to receive different types of technologies. The categories have been updated since the Cold War but reflect the uncertainties of future world politics. Nearly all sensitive decisions are made on a case-by-case basis. Some exceptions to this are made for groups of products that might be related to a single sale, such as spare parts for an aircraft. Not surprisingly, industry complains that decisions are not consistent across purchasers or across technologies.

Although much has been done to loosen the regulations governing the transfer of technologies—especially in the area of computers—industry continues to press for reduced controls and a speedier, more consistent process. Exporting firms try to avoid being denied licenses and will informally "scout" for an answer before proceeding. On the purchasing end of the transaction, end users who are denied access to a particular item have difficulty recovering from being branded as "bad."

As mentioned above, within the DoD itself, technology transfer is a complex process. Potential transfers can be generated by both internal and external requests. They may arise from the Services (each of which differs internally in handling these requests), the Defense Security Assistance Agency, or prospective purchasers. Notably, the objectives of requesters may be at odds with the objectives of other parts of the DoD. Given the potential risk to U.S. troops of advanced weaponry in the hands of an opponent, the DoD is allowed to comment on all proposed exports of defense-related items or technologies. DoD delegates some authority to Commerce for dual-use items exported to certain classes of users. The Defense Technology Security Agency coordinates DoD input to the eventual licensing decision with the departments of State or Commerce. DTSA, as an arm of the Under Secretary of Defense for Policy, has a difficult position reconciling differing views.

Many competing objectives are seen in this arms and technology transfer process. Within the DoD, for example, the Services may propose weapon transfers to enhance allied interoperability. Other common objectives for sales are to reduce the cost of systems to the United States or to maintain some part of the defense industrial base. Foreign governments also exert pressure to be allowed to purchase top-line U.S. equipment and technology.

Each agency within the interagency process typically represents only one of these frequently competing objectives. The State Department may support transfers of weapons and technology as part of their orchestrated support of particular nations. Historically, the ACDA often opposed sales of weapons and technology transfers that were supported by other agencies. In the past, ACDA seemed to be the most conservative agency when it came to approval of arms and technology exports, perhaps because it did not face the competing demands felt by other agencies. ACDA had purely an arms control perspective; economic effects were not part of its organizational objectives. ACDA also had the weakest voice of those around the table and primarily influenced big items meriting congressional approval. How its voice will fare with its consolidation into the Department of State is unclear.

The competing objectives are resolved through the interagency process. This process provides a managerial system for debating individual sales and is also a forum for debating and setting general policies. As such, it has a well-defined "appeal" process, whereby successively higher bureaucratic levels are involved if the lower levels cannot reach agreement. Ultimately, the secretaries of State, Commerce, and Defense would debate an issue and, if they disagreed, send it on to the President. The pressure to avoid raising an issue to such a level provides an important incentive for compromise and agreement at the lower levels. Not surprisingly, given these incentives, only a few license applications—the most problematic—consume the vast bulk of the interagency attention.

Several parallels are apparent between this interagency process and any potential one involving the economic aspects of technology transfer. First, just as the two existing export control processes each have a common purpose, multiple agencies face at least one common problem: the determination of reciprocity or of the level playing field. The various statutes we examined that authorize cooperative agreements all demand at least an agency determination of openness of the national programs in another nation whenever a foreign-owned firm applies. Coordination among agencies would avoid duplicative effort and also ensure equal treatment across agencies. Second, there is the useful involvement of many agencies, such as the intelligence community or the Department of State, which are not automatically involved now. Third, there is a clear design parallel, with the Executive Office of the President overseeing a process involving (in principle) appeals at higher levels.

There are also important differences. First, no single law involves all the agencies. Rather, each agency would come into such a process with its own, unique legislative constraints. To the degree these differ, this argues for an agency-specific process, which is what we have now. Second, the different agencies would not be expressing some opinion on each application, even in principle. Unlike the existing process, in which the participating agencies each express a particular viewpoint, these agencies would tend to have more common, or disinterested, perspectives. The State Department and DoD each have strong views on arms sales to the Middle East; NIH and NASA are unlikely to care strongly about each others' transfers, although they do have useful information to share. Finally, there would be no obvious international system, such as the Coordinating Committee for Multilateral Export Controls was or the Wassenaar Arrangement is, that would in some sense match the U.S. national process.

POLICY IMPLICATIONS

Our analysis of agency policies for controlling international technology transfer suggests that the current set of policies is reasonably effective within its limited scope. There is some evidence that current policy works and no evidence to the contrary.

Still, some small changes in the law and policy might improve the situation. One is granting authority to create "trade secret"–type intellectual property at NASA, perhaps at NIH and within the DoD as well. Currently at NASA, such information must be disclosed, and so its benefit cannot be restricted to U.S. firms. Second is expanding the Bayh-Dole Act requirement for "substantial"

U.S. use of a patent when used for sales in the United States to include *assignments* of patents, in addition to simple licenses. Currently, while a U.S. firm might not be able to license a patent to a foreign firm, the U.S. firm may be bought by that same foreign firm and then assign its licenses to that firm. While entirely legal, this appears to circumvent the intent of the act. Third, an interagency effort could coordinate the reciprocity demands of the various cooperative agreements, perhaps suggesting common definitions or even suggesting changes in some laws.

By contrast, larger policy initiatives that might at first appear attractive in fact pose problems. For example, mandating that agencies track personal interactions for monitoring technology transfer would require an enormous investment of dollars and manpower and has little realistic potential for yielding useful information. At the same time, such activity could inhibit desirable domestic transfers. Likewise, creating a large-scale interagency process for controlling international transfers might appear desirable because it could allow consideration of diplomatic and other issues in allowing foreign firm participation in cooperative agreements. However, in the absence of changes in the underlying laws, the constraints are different for each agency. Such heterogeneity argues against a large interagency process.

Chapter Four

INTERNATIONAL INSIGHTS

Comparing the policies of the United States with those of other advanced nations can suggest alternative approaches to questions of the international transfer of technology. First, we must understand the different situation other nations find themselves in. The United States is unique in the scale of its research enterprise. Some in the United States even see its internal, national developments as completely dominant in all fields. To provide some context, we discuss that perception in comparison to the other OECD nations. This comparison consequently does not consider the R&D expenditures for China and Russia, which may be significant in defense and space. We believe that, in the main, those Russian and Chinese R&D efforts are not competitive with U.S. developments. We found that

- The United States is likely to dominate developments in defense, in which the United States accounts for 72 percent of government-funded military R&D within the OECD.

- This is, perhaps, also true in space systems, in which the U.S. civil space R&D is 58 percent of the total civil, space-related R&D in the OECD nations, and in health and the environment, where the U.S. share is 59 percent.

- It is, however, not true for "economic development R&D," in which the U.S. share is 27 percent (OECD, 1995, pp. 46–49).

The numbers are calculated for the last relatively complete year of OECD data, which is 1993, and use purchasing-power parity. An exception is the calculation for space; there, the last year's estimate of the budget percentage is only available for 1992. We used those percentages, which had changed little in previous years, to estimate the percentage of the 1993 expenditures. For space, only the *civil* expenditures are counted. The large military investments in the United States would further increase the ratio above. Finally, note that these numbers represent only the total government budget appropriations (or outlays) and so do not include private-sector investments. This is probably important in interpreting the full national share of R&D for economic development.

The numbers above still reflect the investment intentions of the national governments.

These comparisons also affect the perceptions and decisions of the other nations. In contrast to the United States, none of the other nations approaches dominance in any area of R&D. In our conversations with Washington representatives of the United Kingdom, the EC, and Japan, the representatives expressed a consistent feeling that their nations must reach out to other nations to tap new technologies; they could not rely upon internal developments alone. The emphasis was thus on understanding what was going on elsewhere in the world and on transferring it successfully to their national firms. Restricting the access of others to their technologies was considered overtly only when national security, in the older, narrow sense, was involved. Otherwise, the transfers were avowedly not an issue of concern.

An extreme case of this dependence on the world can be found in a country we did not investigate directly, the Netherlands. The Netherlands is unusual in the scope of its dependence on international trade; both its imports and its exports are on the order of half its gross domestic product. Perhaps as a consequence, one review of the Dutch policies on science and technology, speaking of fields in which the Dutch had historically been leaders, concluded that

> Maintaining this leadership and capturing the economic benefits from this R&D will increasingly be dependent upon knowledge of, and responsiveness to international developments in these fields. Strengthening international collaboration with scientists will maintain this leadership. Strengthening linkages with international markets through cooperation and collaboration with industry will help secure the potential economic benefits. (OECD, 1987, p. 88.)

For all the nations we discuss, we did not attempt to assess whether the actions of the various countries match such declared positions. It is possible that the actions of other nations are inconsistent with their announced policy, attempting, for example, to restrict access to those technologies developed within their national borders. Such actions are difficult to disentangle from cultural or other barriers to cooperation, even in principle. In practice, we found little hard information on any such activities, much as we found little on espionage. While we cannot rule out such attempts to limit the access to foreigners, the outreach activities attempting to tap technologies from other countries is a real emphasis, presumably reflecting a governmental perception of the problem.

These responses also are consistent with what is reported by others. In one comparison of the United States with Japan, France, Germany, and the United Kingdom, the authors noted the emphasis in France, Germany, and Japan of technology transfer as a "process" rather than as an "event" (Olk and Xin, 1997, pp. 711–728). To us, this reflects a concern with a continual, ongoing effort to increase economic performance, rather than with the particular items produced in any one interaction.

This differing view produces some clear, notable differences in other nations as well. Because of the greater importance of the economic goals for technology development, the federal laboratories in several other countries had technology transfer to their industry as their most important mission—in contrast to the United States and the United Kingdom.

In other matters, there is great commonality among all of these nations. Various sorts of industrial-governmental cooperative agreements seem to be found in all the nations. These are generally targeted at aiding the economies of the nations supporting the agreement. The nations also all use patent licensing as one of the major ways to transfer technology. In the non-U.S. cases, there is also extensive support from the government laboratories for the commercialization of an innovation licensed from the government (Olk and Xin, 1997, pp. 717–719). They also all use the contractual agreements to aid transfer and to involve many researchers in personnel exchanges.

From our conversations, we found a more nuanced set of differences among the nations, as well as some more similarities. In the United Kingdom, we found a clear worldview. The predominant feeling is that the "good stuff" in technology is "out there" somewhere. The problems the United Kingdom faces are

- finding that "good stuff" in the first place

- having a research base that can understand the innovations elsewhere

- making the rest of the United Kingdom's innovation system function well.

Most governmental attention in the United Kingdom has seemingly focused on the last point—on making the taxation and regulatory environment conducive to entrepreneurship. The issues that were the focus of agency attention in the United States—patent licensing and restrictions on cooperative agreements—were not even discussed. In fact, as recounted to us in conversations, the government of the United Kingdom has no written policy on the control of the international transfer of technologies for economic, as opposed to military, grounds.

Our conversations with the EC representatives emphasized the interaction of the EC programs with national ones. The EC research budget is smaller than the national ones, so it aims at leveraging the larger, national efforts.[1] And

---

[1]One example of such an aim is found in EC (1994), p. 22.

indeed, by providing a Europe-wide label to an effort, the efforts of the EC do influence the programs of the individual nations. The overall picture was much the same as that of the United Kingdom; individual European nations understand that a majority of research is occurring in other countries. This leads to attempts to tap the results elsewhere and to an emphasis on making each individual nation "hospitable" to entrepreneurship and innovation (EC, 1994, p. 81 ff.).

The EC does, however restrict the involvement of firms from nonmember nations in their programs. The standard contract for the EC includes a restriction on the participation of third parties. Essentially, the standard contract annex specifies that the commission must approve any subcontract outside of the community before its signing, with few exceptions.[2] The definition of ownership hinges on the ownership or control of a majority of the shares or share equivalents.[3] This excludes U.S. firms unless, on a case-by-case basis, they are approved. The ownership of the patentable innovations on work financed entirely by the EC lodges with the commission, while that from cofinanced work lodges with the participating contractors. The actual use of that information is less restricted. While the community has a right to patent and assume title if the firm fails to file for patents, the contractors must in general only "protect the . . . information which could be used for industrial or commercial application."[4] Importantly, even if the contractor involved has allowed the EC to own any patent, they retain the right to grant nonexclusive sublicenses "necessary in the framework of patent cross-licensing arrangements or technology transfers undertaken by the *Contractor* in its normal course of business."[5] If patented by the firm, the exploitation of the results must simply be "in the interest of the Community."[6] These terms appear to allow many ways for European contractors to transfer such technologies if they so choose.

At least some of the monitoring of the intellectual property created in the EC programs matches this intellectual structure. In some analyses of the BRITE program, the EC appears not even to track intellectual property in the same way that the federal agencies must. Rather, their analyses concentrate on the health of the firms that were involved in the program. In part, this emphasis may be

---

[2]Annex II—General Conditions, Part A—Implementation of the Work, Article 3—Participation of Third Parties.

[3]Annex II—General Conditions, Part A—Implementation of the Work, Article 1—Definitions.

[4]Annex II—General Conditions, Part B—Publicity, Exploitation, and Transfer of Ownership, Article 9—Ownership and Patents.

[5]Annex II—General Conditions, Part B—Publicity, Exploitation, and Transfer of Ownership, Article 9—Ownership and Patents.

[6]Annex II—General Conditions, Part B—Publicity, Exploitation, and Transfer of Ownership, Article 12—General Principles for the Use of Results, and Technology, and Granting *Access Rights.*

that this behavior is the only easy way to deal with intra-European competition. Otherwise, there would be the potential for each country to ask whether they had kept "their" property. Whether that hypothesis is correct or not, though, the clear emphasis we saw in the European programs was on promotion of the ability to innovate, rather than on protecting a stake in individual technical innovations.

These differences between the United States and Europe are hardly confined to technology transfer issues. Rather, they are also symptomatic of deeper and more profound differences. As some commentators have summarized,

> There are basic differences in American and European approaches to the state and the market. Additionally, these differences have had and continue to have consequences for the way in which American and European governments approach problems, interact with each other, and seek to construct the larger Western order. (Benjamin, Quigley, and Neu, 1993, p. 12.)

These differences range from the different origins of regulation of network industries in the two regions—growing out of the authority of state power in Europe but out of competitive markets in the United States—to the differing conceptions of the public trust and the social contract. These differences manifest themselves in many contentious ways quite far from technology policy, such as the protection of "cultural" industries in Canada under the North American Free Trade Agreement. And indeed, the EC has sought similar protections from American culture (Kudrle, 1993, p. 130).

When the focus is on the technology policy, however, the differences manifest themselves in ways similar to the outline we have sketched above. The one difference involving technology, noted by a commentator viewing these overall differences, is in the participation in cooperative agreements of various sorts. In Europe, EC-wide consortia, such as ESPRIT or Eureka, do require the activity to take place in Europe, just as do many U.S. programs. The difference was in comparison with other U.S. programs, such as Sematech or the Partnership for a New Generation of Vehicles, in which the participants have all, in addition, been U.S. firms (Kudrle, 1993, p. 132). This seems not to have occurred in European efforts. This European behavior is consistent with the emphasis we found on the health of the firms involved and neither on details of the ownership nor on the licensing of the intellectual property.

Japan is the other nation usually compared to the United States. In general, and as shown in the OECD compilation, Japanese R&D is focused on economic gains more than research in the United States (OECD, 1995, p. 48). For understanding the restrictions placed upon international technology transfer, though, the social system of allocating the research monies is more important than their comparative amount. Our discussion is based on informal meetings with representatives of the Japanese government. In keeping with the generally important role of nongovernmental bodies in Japanese society, the representative was actually with the New Energy and Industrial Technology Development Organization (NEDO), a "semigovernmental organization under the ministry of International Trade and Industry." (NEDO, n.d. b, p. 1.) NEDO explicitly aims to coordinate the activities of private firms and the public sector. Some documents were provided by the contact in Washington, but these focus almost exclusively on the technical aims of the programs and on facilities and laboratories (NEDO, 1995; NEDO, n.d. a, b, and c). The documents do not describe the process of designing the programs or the role of private firms in that design.

The Japanese system is evidently characterized by intensive involvement of firms early in the design of government R&D efforts. Before the Japanese government has committed funds, the various governmental agencies that will be funding any program negotiate an understanding of the research program with the private entities involved. The key role of private firms is often mediated through a consortium or through an existing industry association. The question of which firms can be involved in such a consultative group is perplexing to some in Japan, just as it is here. Is Mazda, now effectively controlled by Ford, a Japanese company? The apparent response is "yes," at least for now.

The implicit opening of such groups to all Japanese firms avoids one issue that is troublesome in the United States. That is equity—or choosing which firms the national government should help. This arrangement also provides an easily arguable linkage to economic growth. Since the firms involved from the start are Japanese, the benefits should naturally accrue to Japan. This also implicitly handles all the difficult-to-measure forms of technology transfer, by limiting the participants at the start. Finally, this arrangement also facilitates the transfer to the firms, since they are involved from the start of a program.

Formal controls on patents are maintained. An important difference between the Japanese and American treatment of patents is the Japanese practice of keeping full or, in the newer programs, half ownership of any resulting patent in governmental hands. In this arrangement, the Japanese government always knows the licensees for any patent in which it has invested and, in fact, has the ownership right of refusing a prospective licensee. They do not, however, track whether a co-owner or licensee of a patent is in fact using it, unlike the attention focused in the United States on march-in rights.

Other forms of intellectual property, such as trade secrets, are not emphasized. Those we have talked with insist that there are no comprehensive data in Japan, even on the disposition of patents, let alone on the more diffuse forms of intellectual property.

Overall, the picture drawn here of the Japanese system is quite a contrast with the U.S. system. The Japanese seem more focused on the firms involved with governmental programs than on the intellectual property the programs produce. The firms, and their health, are the aim of the programs. The intellectual property is simply a means to the end of economic gain for the firms and thus, indirectly, for Japan. The firms are also, evidently, trusted to exploit the intellectual property with little oversight.

Other countries view international technology transfer differently from how the United States does. Their common view emphasizes reaching out for technology and making their nation or region more hospitable to innovation and does not emphasize controls. The controls that do exist focus more on access to cooperative programs than on controlling intellectual property. This is partly a consequence of their smaller domestic research efforts, but it partly also recognizes the worldwide spread of research.

Almost certainly, the United States should similarly emphasize other aspects of innovation as well. In many areas of economically important technology development, the rest of the world invests amounts larger than or comparable to those in the United States, so outreach is almost certainly needed. Additionally, the United States must keep this international perspective in mind when fashioning any diplomatic initiatives, such as negotiations for common restrictions on access to cooperative agreements.

Chapter Five

A BRIEF OBSERVATION FROM THE COMMERCIAL WORLD

These observations from a limited set of international comparisons parallel a position also expressed in the United States. In the United States, private industry has also evolved a different construction of the problem. Intellectual property is now widely viewed as another strategic asset, to be managed by a company just as it manages its financial assets or its physical or human capital (Hamilton, 1997, pp. 163–176). Each company understands that it rarely owns all the technologies needed for a commercial success, just as it previously realized the need for partners in design, distribution, or sales. As such, technology becomes an important asset available to be traded for the right "price"—perhaps access to other, complementary technology or access to a foreign market. Just as in our foreign examples, the focus is on the advantage to the individual firm, not on the technology per se.

This evolving commercial worldview has several observable consequences. First, there is a growth in strategic alliances of various sorts, both within national borders and across them. Whether a formal joint venture is formed or a more limited interaction occurs, such as cross-licensing of patents, such relationships are formed daily. Often, this is described as being related to "virtual" corporations, in which alliances shift with the needs of the moment. In another view, these alliances are longer-term and reflect the increased complexity of modern technology and the need for local marketing and distribution, if not local content as well.

Second, the management of intellectual property, which is largely confined to patents, is also much more visible today. Particularly in the various parts of the information technology industry, there appear to be more, and more vigorous, patent infringement suits in the United States. The recent, highly visible suit and countersuit between Intel and DEC is just the most recent case in point. The negotiated settlement of that case is also typical, as these suits, and the management of the intellectual property, are now just another lever in commercial competition.

This emerging worldview, focusing on firms, not on technologies, is not restricted to private firms. A recent report from the Kennedy School has a similar philosophy (Branscomb et al., 1997). In that report, the authors recognize the key role of the private sector in investing in new technologies for economic gains. Their view thus emphasizes the results for firms rather than the development or transfer of technologies. They also, much as our foreign comparisons do, emphasize the use of "all policy tools, not just R&D support" and note the need for U.S. firms to "get maximum benefit from world-wide sources of innovation." (Branscomb et al., 1997.)

This emerging world view in the United States may shift the U.S. position away from its historical one. As Olk and Xin (1997, p. 711) say, "Traditionally, the USA has been the generator of technology and concerned with limiting transfer." That may well change as we enter the twenty-first century, with the United States adopting a policy stance more similar to that of the other, smaller, but technically advanced nations.

Chapter Six

POTENTIAL CHANGES IN INTERNATIONAL TECHNOLOGY TRANSFER POLICIES AND PROCEDURES

Overall, the international transfer of technologies in which the federal government has invested is a complex public policy issue. First, the issue can be politically charged. Whenever U.S. efforts are seen as benefiting firms in other nations, some will object. A recent example is the debate involving the extreme ultraviolet consortium, primarily consisting of Intel; Advanced Micro Devices; Motorola; and Sandia, Lawrence Berkeley, and Los Alamos National Laboratories. The issue there is the potential transfer of the advanced lithography technologies to the Japanese firms of Canon and Nikon and the Dutch firm ASM Lithography (Leopold, 1997).

Second, as our economic analysis indicated, the effects of many transfer mechanisms are hard to estimate, even in principle. More importantly, since the same hard-to-estimate methods operate internally in the United States and we must rely on them to justify the federal investment in the first place, we should be wary of any monitoring or other efforts that might tend to discourage such transfers.

Finally, as our investigations of the different agencies showed, a multiplicity of laws and regulations constrains actions here. While some programs apply across agencies almost without exception, such as the Bayh-Dole provisions, each agency has some unique constraints beyond the shared ones. In general, the statements of the agency representatives and our investigations into their practice all indicated that the agencies are attempting to comply with all the constraints and are largely succeeding.

This complexity, and the largely successful efforts of the agencies to deal with their immediate problems, argues for no sweeping changes. Nonetheless, several smaller changes are suggested in the discussions of individual agencies. These fall under several categories—investigating other modes of transfer, further restrictions on patent transfers, enhancement of the ability of the federal agencies to protect potential trade secrets, and coordination of the policy and determinations for international participation in cooperative programs. We will briefly discuss each of these in turn.

GATHERING INFORMATION

One obvious alternative would be to address the information deficiencies concerning the many unmonitored methods of technology transfer. This would require that the federal agencies expand the data presently gathered. This would most probably include information on personnel movements of those involved with government research. It could also demand information on the technologies being shared in joint ventures or other alliances potentially involving government research, although the firms involved would surely object. Other expansions could be imagined as well, such as attempts to quantify international industrial espionage.

The difficulty with these methods is that they would all require a great deal of effort, both on the part of the government and on the part of the private entities. Even ignoring potential privacy concerns or proprietary information, the load would be great.

At the same time, the information would *still* not suffice to follow the international transfers of technology. The actual sharing of information within a joint venture can never be clear from the outside. Other methods, such as reverse engineering and (most probably) espionage, would remain highly uncertain.

Most important, given the caution from our economic analysis to avoid unintentional harm to domestic technology transfer, all of these data-gathering efforts seem worrisome. While we cannot estimate the likelihood of actually interfering with such desirable transfers, it is easy to imagine a tendency to avoid actions that might trigger these reports. These high costs and weak benefits seem to make this option unattractive.

PATENTS

Our discussion of the DoE would suggest amending the Bayh-Dole patent restrictions to include the assignment of rights. This would allow the restrictions on the use of a patent to follow its assignment, not just its licensing.

On its face, this seems a simple change in keeping with the spirit of the original law. On the other hand, the firms that have such patents would see this as restricting their freedom to dispose of themselves and, thus, a diminution of the value of the firm. Given the small number of such cases, the aggregate economic importance of this change is certainly small. The issue is more one of fairness, which is fundamentally a political judgment.

TRADE SECRETS

The issue with trade secrets came up in conjunction with NASA. There, government employees have created trade secret–type intellectual property. However, under the Space Act and the Freedom of Information Act, NASA is unable to properly protect such property, which devolves to the public; as such, it is available to all companies, foreign and domestic.

One clear need is to query all the agencies on need for legal authority. We found no such cases outside of NASA, but the potential is there whenever government employees do research. Presumably, this would be followed by proposed changes in the authorizing statutes for the necessary agencies, much like the changes NASA has proposed.

Additionally, it may be reasonable to direct the development of procedures fitting the requirements of the federal espionage law within these agencies, even before the statutory authority to protect this class of information. Such procedures are needed legally. In their absence, information can be legally deemed to have been compromised and is thus ineligible for protection as a trade secret. Given the long lead times needed to implement such procedures, an early start seems reasonable.

Finally, one subject that we did not investigate in depth may be of interest. The ownership of trade secrets at the DoE laboratories, many of which are run by large corporations, seems an unexplored issue. Currently, any trade secrets produced at a laboratory are simply the property of the contractor running the laboratory. It is not clear whether such corporations are the most appropriate or efficient owners of such intellectual property. A study of alternative arrangements for the ownership of such trade secrets might suggest changes in those contracts.

COOPERATIVE AGREEMENTS

The final area of potential action is the creation of common, or at least coordinated, language and decisions on cooperative agreements. This would most easily be accomplished under an organized interagency process for the international aspects of technology transfer. Presumably, this would be organized under the NSTC and modeled on the existing defense-related process for export review, run under the NSC staff.

The primary task for such a process would be to develop common reciprocity or level-playing-field access requirements for R&D programs. Ideally, these could be coordinated with any diplomatic actions attempting an international coordination of such requirements (Branscomb et al., 1997). If this were the only task, however, the natural structure would be an ad hoc committee rather than a standing process.

The same process could also be used to monitor the application of the requirements with the active involvement of the departments of State and Commerce and of the Office of Science and Technology Policy. This would avoid the current model, in which each agency independently decides whether a particular foreign nation fits the agency's criteria. Particularly if the criteria are consistent across agencies, this would avoid inconsistent rulings. On the one hand, this appears to be a national decision and so would benefit from a coordinated decision process. On the other, it may be prudent to allow such decisions to be made at low levels, precisely to avoid drawing attention to them. Currently, the profusion of differing laws specific to individual agencies prevents easy consistency and so makes an interagency process for application of the policy less compelling.

Finally, any such interagency process could also oversee any of the data gathering suggested above, such as information on the need in different agencies for the ability to protect trade-secret sorts of information. While this seems insufficient in itself to motivate the creation of such a process, it would best be done under such a coordinated system.

Agmon, Marcy, James L. Bonomo, Michael Kennedy, Maren Leed, Kenneth Watman, Katharine Webb, and Charles Wolf, Jr., *Arms Proliferation Policy: Support to the Presidential Advisory Board*, Santa Monica, Calif.: RAND, MR-771-OSD, 1996.

Benjamin, Roger, Denise D. Quigley, and C. R. Neu, eds., *Balancing State Intervention: The Limits of Transatlantic Markets*, New York: St. Martin's Press, 1993.

Branscomb, Lewis, Richard Florida, David Hart, James Keller, and Darin Boville, Investing in Innovation, Toward a Consensus Strategy for Federal Technology Policy, dated April 24, 1997. Accessed November 13, 1997, at **http://www.ksg.harvard.edu/iip/techproj/invest.html**

Dalton, Donald H., and Manuel G. Serapio, Jr., *Globalizing Industrial Research and Development*, Department of Commerce, Office of Technology Policy, Asia-Pacific Technology Program, October 1995.

Department of Commerce, Bureau of Export Administration, *Critical Technology Assessment of the U.S. Optoelectronics Industry*, February 1994.

European Commission, *Growth, Competitiveness, Employment: The Challenges and Ways Forward Into the 21st Century*, white paper, Luxembourg: Office for Official Publications of the European Communities, 1994.

Fehner, Terrence R., and Jack M. Holl, The United States Department of Energy, 1977–1994, A Summary History. Accessed October 27, 1997, at **http://www.doe.gov/html/doe/about/history/doehist.html#ZZ2**

Foster Associates, *A Survey of Net Rates of Return on Innovations, Washington*, D.C.: National Science Foundation, 1978.

Washington, D.C., National Science Foundation, 1978.Hamilton, William F., "Managing Technology as a Strategic Asset," *International Journal of Technology Management*, Vol. 14, Nos. 2/3/4, 1997, pp. 163–176.

Hightower, Jud, Department of Energy, private letter, August 13, 1997.

Jaffe, Adam B., "Technological Opportunity and Spillovers of R&D: Evidence from Firms' Patents, Profits, and Market Value," *The American Economic Review*, Vol. 76, No. 5, December 1986.

Kiefer, Rodney D., Deputy Director, Industrial Partnerships and Commercialization, Lawrence Livermore National Laboratory, private letter, August 28, 1997.

Kudrle, Robert T., "Markets, Governments, and Policy Congruence," in Roger Benjamin, Denise D. Quigley, and C. R. Neu, eds., *Balancing State Intervention: The Limits of Transatlantic Markets*, New York: St. Martin's Press, 1993.

Leopold, George, "EUV Litho Effort Hits Political Snag Over Foreign Ties," *EE Times*, October 21, 1997. Accessed November 30, 1997, at **http:// techweb.cmp.com/eet/news/97/977news/euv.html**

Lorell, Mark, *Troubled Partnership: A History of U.S.-Japan Collaboration on the FS-X Fighter*, Santa Monica, Calif.: RAND, MR-612/2-AF, 1995.

Mansfield, Edwin, John Rapoport, Anthony Romeo, Samuel Wagner, and George Beardsley, "Social and Private Rates of Return from Industrial Innovations," *Quarterly Journal of Economics*, Vol. 91, No. 2, May 1977.

Mansfield, Edwin, et al., *Technology Transfer, Productivity, and Economic Policy*, 1st ed., New York: Norton, 1982.

Mowery, David C., and Nathan Rosenberg, "The Commercial Aircraft Industry," in Richard R. Nelson, ed., *Government and Technical Progress*, New York: Pergamon Press, 1982.

NASA—*see* National Aeronautics and Space Administration.

National Academy of Sciences, National Academy of Engineering, Institute of Medicine, Committee on Science, Engineering, and Public Policy, *Finding Common Ground: U.S. Export Controls in a Changed Global Environment, Panel on the Future Design and Implementation of U.S. National Security Export Controls*, Washington, D.C.: National Academy Press, 1991.

National Aeronautics and Space Administration, *NASA Export Control Program (NASA/ECP)*, Draft, March 1997a.

_____, NASA's "Domestic" Commercial Technology Transfer Mission v. International Technology Transfer, presentation to NCTMT, July 15, 1997b.

National Archives and Records Administration, Office of the *Federal Register*, *The United States Government Manual 1996/1997*, reprint, Lanham, Md.: Bernan, September 1996.

National Institute of Standards and Technology, *Optoelectronics at NIST*, Boulder, Colo., NISTIR-5054, 1996.

National Science Board, *Science and Engineering Indicators* 1996, Arlington, Va.: National Science Foundation, NSB-96-21, 1996.

National Science Foundation, *Research & Development in Industry*, Arlington, Va., NSF-96-304, 1993.

_____, *Research & Development in Industry*, Arlington, Va., early release tables, 1994.

NEDO—*see* New Energy and Industrial Technology Development Organization.

New Energy and Industrial Technology Development Organization, "NEDO Creates New Energy," Tokyo, September 1995.

_____, "Global Environmental Technology," Tokyo, undated a.

_____, "New Energy and Industrial Technology Development Organization," Tokyo, undated b.

_____, "New Technology," Tokyo, undated c.

Nolan, Janne E., Edward Randolph Jayne II, Ronald F. Lehman, David E. McGiffert, and Paul C. Warnke, "Report of the Presidential Advisory Board on Arms Proliferation Policy," undated.

NSB—*see* National Science Board.

NSF—*see* National Science Foundation.

OECD—*see* Organization for Economic Cooperation and Development.

Olk, Paul, and Katherine Xin, "Changing the Policy on Government-Industry Cooperative R&D Arrangements: Lessons from the US Effort," *International Journal of Technology Management*, Vol. 13, Nos. 7/8, 1997.

Organization for Economic Cooperation and Development, *Main Science and Technology Indicators*, 1995/1, Paris, 1995.

_____, *Reviews of National Science and Technology Policy: Netherlands*, Paris, France, 1987.

Popper, Steven W., *Economic Approaches to Measuring the Performance and Benefit of Fundamental Science*, Santa Monica: RAND, MR-708.0-OSTP, 1995.

Reid, Proctor P., and Alan Schriesheim, eds., *Foreign Participation in U.S. Research and Development: Asset or Liability*, Washington, D.C.: National Academy Press, 1996a.

_____, *Prospering in a Global Economy: Foreign Participation in U.S. Research and Development,* Washington, D.C.: National Academy Press, 1996b.

Robert R. Nathan Associates, *Net Rates of Return on Innovations,* Washington, D.C., National Science Foundation, 1978.

The White House, *A National Security Strategy of Engagement and Enlargement,* February 1995.